PEDAL CAR
Restoration and Price Guide

Andrew G. Gurka

Published by

krause
publications

700 E. State Street • Iola, WI 54990-0001
Telephone: 715/445-2214

Please call or write for our free catalog.
Our toll-free number to place an order or obtain a free catalog is 800-258-0929
or please use our regular business telephone 715-445-2214 for editorial comment
and further information.

Library of Congress Catalog Number: 95-82423
ISBN: 0-87341-405-5

Printed in the United States of America

To my son Kyle

A portion of the author's proceeds have gone
to support the special needs of autistic children.

CONTENTS

CONTENTS

ACKNOWLEDGMENTS

Special thanks to:
>
> John Rastall, collector and publisher of *The Wheel Goods Trader*
>
> Bobby Alford, author of *History of Murray Ohio*
>
> John Gunnell, automotive history author
>
> Art Lieskinen, collector
>
> Dave Harrington, pedal car restorer
>
> Bob Ellsworth, owner of Pedal Car Graphics
>
> International Paint Stripping, Mark Kochanoski, Manager
>
> C & J Fastener
>
> Fairlane Welding, Joe Lipani, Master Welder
>
> Model Paint Company, Thomas Schramm, Formulator
>
> Van Eden, owner of Pedal Car Accessory's
>
> Allen Wilson, owner of Cowboys & Kidillacs
>
> Boy Toys Inc., owner Bill Hampton
>
> Samuelson Pedal Tractor Parts
>
> Cliff and Lucy Cooney, owners of Pedal Car Kid's
>
> Rick Braekevelt
>
> Robert Hann
>
> Jim Dodge
>
> Jeff Balog
>
> Ralph Brown
>
> Don Lawrence
>
> Leonard Gurka
>
> Stephen Gurka
>
> Eugene Steward
>
> Thomas Houle
>
> John Klovski

ACKNOWLEDGMENTS

Additional thanks to:

Anderson Public Library

Antiques & The Arts Weekly, Laura Beach, Feature Writer

Arlyce Amrhien, Vice President and General Manager of MTD

Autoknow

Olney Public Library

Toledo/Lucas County Library, Donna, Local History Librarian

Cleveland Public Library, Joan L. Clark, Head Librarian

Detroit Automotive Historical Collection

Detroit Public Library, Marion Rodgers, Librarian

Elkhart Public Library

Henry Ford Museum, Marlene Manseau, Marketing and Public Relations

Henry Ford Museum Research Library, Linda Skolarus, Access Services

Mead Public Library, Roberta K. May, Librarian

Noel Barrett Antiques & Auctions Ltd.

Sandwich Auction House

Tiffin-Seneca Public Library, Jane B. Wickham, Librarian

I'd also like to thank my wife Janine for her word processing assistance and patience while I was writing this book.

INTRODUCTION

"Wow, is that thing neat!" "Hey, look at the little car! I had one exactly like that as a kid!" These are the typical responses that one hears from folks when they see an old pedal car. Almost instantly, a flood of nostalgic feelings and a swirl of old memories are brought to their minds. For a moment, no longer are they concerned with the problems of the present; they're busy recalling the times as a child when they played with a pedal car, wagon, or scooter and sold lemonade on their street. The pedal car will forever be equated with childhood and that golden age of innocence.

The intent of this book is to offer the collector and restorer a wide range of useful information about pedal cars. Begin by delving into why pedal cars are universally admired and have become true collectors' items. Continue pedaling along and discover the history of pedal car manufacturers, never before told, gleaned from old articles and rare literature. Trace automotive history as the pedal car evolved along with full-size cars. To help those interested in fixing up their pedal car, a special section on restoration is included. The principles shown can be applied to most any type of pedal vehicle. As a bonus, a current price guide has been compiled for informational use by collectors and enthusiasts.

Many of the wonderful illustrations, advertisements, and original catalog pages that appear in this book were made available by John Rastall. John is one of the country's largest collectors of pedal car literature. He owns many rare catalogs and has a sizable collection of pedal cars, wagons, and old toys.

As publisher of *Wheel Goods Trader*, he offers pedal car enthusiasts an interesting and informative monthly magazine. Hats off to John for his cooperation in making this book possible and for his continuing contributions to the pedal car hobby.

*Restored 1961 Speedway Pace Car by Murray
Ohio*

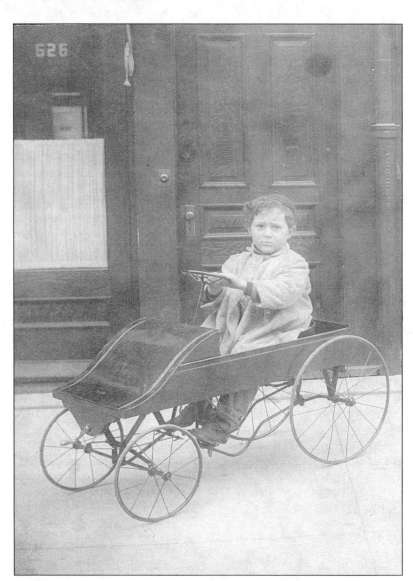

*A typical example of an early pedal car. Note the
spoked wheels, the curved pedal rods, and the hand
crank. This little boy has a concerned look on his
face, probably because he had to stop playing and
pose for a photograph. (Courtesy John Rastall)*

Section I

The Appeal, Design and History of the

PEDAL CAR

During WWII the country needed a little comic relief. The appeal of the pedal car was enough that a national magazine choose to run an illustration of one on its cover. (Courtesy John Rastall)

CHAPTER 1

THE FASCINATION OF THE PEDAL CAR

Pedal cars, juvenile automobiles, play vehicles, wheel goods, and kiddie cars—all are names that have been used to describe a group of pedal-powered toy vehicles that were ridden and enjoyed by children, especially in the United States. A modest number of lucky individuals can remember having a pedal car as a child or playing with one at a friend's house. Others can recall merely pressing their noses against a storefront window many years ago to get a better view of a shiny new pedal car.

"Pedal car" usually refers to a child's toy vehicle with pedals, wheels, tires, axles, body, and steering assembly. Pedal cars were designed for heavy play outdoors and many were treated roughly or left to the elements year round, which accounts for the less than pristine condition that most are in today. Scores of pedal cars underwent "backyard restorations" that altered their original appearance.

Geared for children two to six years of age, juvenile vehicles were pedaled around on sidewalks, alleys, and driveways all across the United States. Prior to 1940, pedal cars were purchased largely by wealthy parents for their children. These "rich kids" lived mainly in sprawling homes near large cities. At one time the exclusive subdivisions in Beverly Hills, Long Island, Detroit, Chicago, Boston, Cleveland, and many other cities were pockets of activity for kids and their pedal cars.

Not everyone had the luxury of having affluent parents, however, and many of today's pedal car enthusiasts never owned a pedal car as a child. This is not unusual, as many middle class parents bought their children affordable alternatives like velocipedes, wagons, and scooters. With a little Yankee ingenuity, anything was possible. One of the simplest toy vehicles was a "kart" style car made from discards such as old crates, pallets, and wagon wheels. Even an old garbage can or washtub could be used as a makeshift body. "Tin can headlights" made a good finishing touch. Many a father who couldn't afford to buy his child a pedal car put together one of these homemade

During the 1920s and 1930s it was primarily kids from affluent neighborhoods who owned pedal cars. Seen here are two well-to-do children playing with a pedal car while their "nanny" keeps careful watch from the driveway. This postcard was sent during October of 1929 by a Detroit family who was visiting Hollywood, California. (Courtesy John Rastall)

"sidewalk cruisers." I can recall assembling one of these crude vehicles with my father. After finding some old wood in the garage to construct the body and pirating four wheels from a baby's buggy found in the trash, our car was nearly complete. The steering was accomplished by placing one foot on each side of the front axle and was assisted with a hand-held length of rope. We nailed on a short wooden hand brake that I could engage in an attempt to stop the car, especially when coasting down a steep hill. As a finishing touch we painted the car white using

Not all children who owned pedal cars were rich. Some children played with basic models of pedal cars that were obtained secondhand in less than pristine condition. (Courtesy John Rastall)

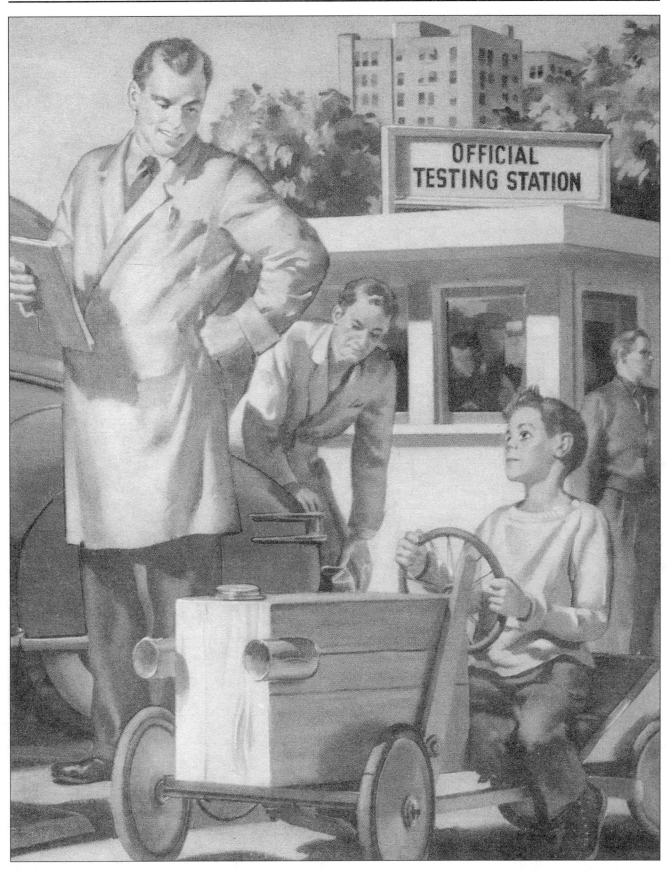

Many homemade cars used an old wood crate to form the front of the body. Note the "tin can headlights" and the friction hand brake. (Courtesy John Rastall)

THE FASCINATION OF THE PEDAL CAR

From an early age, children are curious about the world around them. This baby, although too small to reach the pedals, wanted to try driving. (Courtesy John Rastall)

leftover house paint. For a custom look, we dipped a brush in bright orange paint and spattered it onto the car. The car was a big hit with the neighborhood kids and was the first "automotive" project that I worked on with my father.

Once it was every red-blooded American kid's dream to have his or her very own pedal car; today many adults have that same desire. Pedal car enthusiasts are of all ages and occupations. I know a funeral director who, presumably to es-

Many grown-ups can remember happy times during their childhood when they played with friends in the neighborhood. Even if a child didn't own a pedal car, friends would often share theirs. (Courtesy John Rastall)

A brother and sister shown together on the farm with their pedal car. As children grow up and go their separate ways, they sometimes long for the good old days when they were young. (Courtesy John Rastall)

Not all children who received pedal cars were thrilled with them. This boy's father spent a large portion of his take home pay to buy a Garton Hot Rod. The youngster, Thomas Houle, never really enjoyed playing with the pedal car because his legs were too short to reach the pedals. (Courtesy Thomas Houle)

cape the melancholy environment of his job, retires to his basement to secretly work on restoring pedal cars. Other enthusiasts are retired businessmen, some of whom are millionaires that can indulge in the hobby of collecting and restoring pedal cars to their hearts' content. Still other enthusiasts have turned a hobby into a small business. Over the past several years, various companies have been formed with the sole purpose of providing parts and restorations for pedal cars.

What makes pedal cars so fascinating to children and adults alike? It may stem from the attraction that people have always had to the automobile. This interest in the automobile begins at an early age. As anyone who has raised a child can tell you, babies are very curious about cars. They reach for the keys, try to turn the steering wheel, grab the gearshift lever, and push on the horn button. It's usually at a slightly older age, between two

THE FASCINATION OF THE PEDAL CAR

A doting parent helps one of her children stand on the back of a Pontiac fire truck made by Murray Ohio. This photo was found in the attic of an old house undergoing renovation.

A pedal car can be modified to be an expression of one's individuality. A father embellished this car with reflectors and other ornaments for his handicapped child. (Courtesy John Rastall)

and three, that many children get their first glimpse of a pedal car. When little children see a pedal car for the first time, they do a double take. Their eyes can't believe what they're seeing—a little car just their size. Next comes a mad dash to climb into this new plaything! Once inside, they proceed to try everything out.

Many adults feel a similar excitement when they see or talk about pedal cars. Pedal cars have a way of generating pleasant, nostalgic feelings in grown-ups, especially parents

Some restorers like to customize their pedal cars. This Murray Champion with flames, though not original, is an eye catcher. (Courtesy John Rastall)

and grandparents of young children. When adults see a pedal car, it may bring back fond memories of playing with them as children. Those were carefree times when they played all day long and were with family members who may now be gone. Pedal cars bring out the child that has been tucked away inside of them. In a sense, the fascination of the pedal car allows grown-ups to recapture their lost youth and remember what innocence was.

For sentimental reasons, people will often store old pedal cars in an attic, basement, barn, or garage for years. Just think of the magnificent old pedal cars that are still waiting to be discovered! Some of these treasures may be in excellent original condition, while others may need to be completely restored. The restoration process can be challenging and at the same time, enjoyable. Part of the excitement of restoring a pedal car is the sense of accomplishment that it brings. Restorers will follow the project from start to finish, from eyesore to heirloom, and will feel great pride while showing the completed pedal car to others.

THE SWITCH TO PEDAL CARS

The number of classic car restorers that are switching to pedal car restorations has been on the rise in recent years. This is occurring due to four main reasons: 1) Pedal cars on average are less expensive to restore than full-size automobiles. Instead of spending thousands on a frame-off restoration of an antique or classic car, some pedal cars can be expertly restored for a few hundred dollars. This cost may be reduced even more if the restorer is willing to do most of the work. However, don't think that all restorations are that inexpensive. A heavily optioned pedal car from the 1930s in need of total restoration could easily end up costing thousands of dollars to restore. 2) The amount of space required for restoration and storage of a pedal car is dramatically smaller than a "real" car. A pedal car need only occupy a small corner of a room instead of a major portion of a garage. Buffs are so pleased with their pedal-powered possessions that they put them in an honored place such as the family room or den. But beware—if you accumulate several large pedal cars you may end up with a storage problem of your own. 3) There is virtually no maintenance on a pedal car. All that is required is a little dusting now and then, versus oil changes, tune-ups, fuel expenses, batteries, and muffler changes. 4) A pedal car restoration calls on many of the same skills, such as bodywork and paintwork, that a full-size automobile does, only on a smaller scale.

Not surprisingly, some pedal cars were created to promote real cars and build goodwill among customers. Car makers felt that if junior could be sold on a certain model of pedal car, dad might be influenced to buy the real thing. Currently, many owners of full-size classic cars are clamoring to buy identical pedal cars to match the types of vehicles they possess. By having a nicely restored pedal car to go along with the full-size version, the collector reinforces his pride and sentiment for his personal choice of vehicle.

A few years ago, a successful real estate agent purchased a full-size 1938 Buick for a reasonable price. After the deal was made and the buyer was leaving, the seller's wife ran out of the house and said, "I almost forgot—this goes with the car." She proceeded to give the buyer an original 1930s Buick American National pedal car. Apparently the seller didn't realize the pedal car he gave away was worth half the value of the full-size Buick he sold.

WHY CAN'T I FIND ANY OLD PEDAL CARS?

Pedal cars have emotional and sentimental appeal that cuts across all age groups and is not affected by race, creed, or color. Many ordinary folks would like to own a pedal car or try their hand at restoring one. Classic car buffs and toy collectors are seeking out pedal cars to enhance their collections; others see the opportunity to buy and resell pedal cars for a profit.

You may wonder why pedal cars are so scarce, since several large companies produced them for a long time. One reason is that although certain wheel goods manufacturers were in business for many years, the actual number of pedal cars sold may have been relatively small in comparison to other less expensive toys the company offered. It is believed that many deluxe versions of pedal cars from the 1920s and 1930s, although appearing in catalogs as stock items, were actually being produced on a special order basis. This meant that the cost of these special order pedal cars was astronomical in comparison to what the average parent might spend on a toy for a child. For example, a deluxe pedal car from the late 1920s would have sold for $60 or more, whereas an ordinary tricycle would have sold for $6.

In addition, several early pedal car companies were only in business a short while and didn't produce very many examples of their product. This observation applies mainly to pre-World War II pedal cars, as those after this period were produced in larger quantities and became more affordable to the average family.

Another reason pedal cars are scarce is that they wore out. They were created to be used by the roughest bunch of individuals to ever roam the planet—kids! Children are famous for their ability to wear out toys, and pedal cars were no exception. Over time the formerly shiny new pedal car would look like a rusty piece of scrap.

Did someone say scrap? This is another important factor that contributed to the scarcity of the pedal car. During the First and Second World Wars the government directed the use of metal in both the public and private sectors. Patriotic citizens organized scrap metal drives that were focused on obtaining scrap iron, steel, and aluminum. Many a school kid from the WWII era can remember combing the streets and alleys for any scrap of metal, including cans, bottlecaps, or even foil gum wrappers. Naturally, since pedal cars were made of steel, many fell prey to the collection efforts of private citizens. If the government thought about it back then, they would have made a propaganda poster that said "Uncle Sam Wants Your Pedal Car." No one will ever know the exact number of pedal cars that were scrapped because of recycling and the war effort, but it would be reasonable to expect that in desperate times when materials were scarce, a sizable percentage of pedal cars were lost.

Another factor contributing to the scarcity of pedal cars was safety conscious parents. Sometimes secondhand pedal cars were discarded by well-meaning parents who felt the toys could pose a safety hazard. Some of the older cars had protruding trim and if the child fell against it an injury could result. Other parents modified the cars by removing hood ornaments and other accessories in order to make them safer. Some parents threw pedal cars out as clutter once their children no longer used them, further contributing to the disappearance of pedal cars over the years.

In some cases, pedal cars were used as incentives for kids to sell magazine subscriptions (Courtesy John Rastall)

Skippy was a popular cartoon character during the 1920s and 1930s. Created by Percy Crosby in 1923, all sorts of toys, including pedal cars, carried the Skippy endorsement. This premium card dated 1933 was packed in a box of Wheaties cereal.

HEALTH BENEFITS OF PEDAL CARS

In the early 1900s, many epidemics, including influenza, polio, and tuberculosis, swept through the United States. Many of the stricken were young children. As the patient recovered, part of the recommended course of treatment often included home remedies, fresh air, sunshine, and mild exercise. Various pedal car manufacturers of that era touted the restorative powers of the pedal car. An ad found in a Spear & Company catalog for an early Buick pedal car states, "Just imagine the days, weeks, and months of muscle-making, health-making fun this car will give your youngster. It will give him sturdy legs, strong stomach muscles, and the rugged vigor that comes with exercise in the open." Parents believed in the pedal car as a way to promote recuperation and to provide their children with an excellent form of exercise. The pedal car was certainly not a panacea for all childhood ailments, but the sheer joy of receiving one and using it on a beautiful sunny day must have been the best kind of medicine.

PEDAL CARS AS ADVERTISING

The public always thought of pedal cars in a favorable manner and other businesses were aware of this early on. From the early 1900s to the present, pedal cars have graced

The popularity of the pedal car was reflected in children's Valentine cards such as this one dated 1942 featuring a Skippy Roadster by Gendron (Courtesy John Rastall)

calendars, postcards, and magazine covers, and have been used in all types of advertising to sell various products. Insurance companies such as Mutual of Omaha liked to show pedal cars in their ads and peppered them in magazines. The colorful illustrations would catch the eye and tie in nicely to the rambling text about insuring the family car. Gasoline companies such as Texaco liked to feature pedal cars in their ads, as did many manufacturers of children's foodstuffs. When one examines old magazine ads, brand names like Ovaltine, Dole pineapple juice, and Cream of Wheat frequently were associated with children in pedal cars. Even General Electric used the positive image of the pedal car to sell washing machines, refrigerators, and air conditioners.

In another marketing strategy, businesses such as department stores would hold a contest in which the winner received a pedal car. It was common for the store to have a

About your family cars and Securance. Securance can't keep a shine on your chrome, but it *can* provide you with the last word in driving protection—through Nationwide Insurance, the choice of over 2¼ million careful drivers. You get broad coverage—as liberal as any anywhere—at fair rates, backed by claims service that's really *fast*. Yet quality car insurance is only *part* of your Securance "package." Securance can also insure your *life, health, family, home* and *property*. All at low cost, with no gaps, overlaps or extras. All through your Nationwide agent, who takes care of all the details for you. Check your Yellow Pages for his name and number.

Securance is all-risk, one agent, "packaged" protection. Covers your life, health, home, car and property. It's available only through your Nationwide agent. He's in the Yellow Pages.

Nationwide Mutual Ins. Co. / Nationwide Life Ins. Co. / Nationwide Mutual Fire Ins. Co. / home office, Columbus, O.

Insurance companies liked to feature pedal cars in their advertising because of the universal appeal of these wheeled toys. It was also an easy tie-in to the family car. The man in the advertisement doesn't appear very cheerful—maybe he just got a quote on insuring his new car. (Courtesy John Rastall)

GUARANTEED
AGAINST ALL SERVICE EXPENSE
for three years..

Now as low as $187. (AT THE FACTORY)

EVERY General Electric Refrigerator is guaranteed for 3 full years against service expense of any kind. This unqualified guarantee is backed by an unparalleled performance record in well over a million homes. It is substantial evidence of the long life of unfailing operation a G-E will give you. All the simple mechanism is sealed in steel in the Monitor Top. It requires no attention—not even oiling. Cabinets are *all*-steel, built for long, sturdy service and lined with acid-resisting porcelain. Sliding shelves afford more readily usable shelf space and bring food within sight and easy reach. The sanitary all-porcelain super-freezer has generous ice cube capacity. These are but a few of the advantages adding greater convenience to a lasting investment. New lower prices make the General Electric a more outstanding value than ever. A complete range of sizes and lowest terms are now available.

Write for a copy of our magazine "The Silent Hostess." It will be sent to you free. Each issue contains delightful recipes, household hints, health talks, entertainment ideas by noted authorities. Address, General Electric Co., Electric Refrigeration Department, Section G5, Hanna Bldg., Cleveland, Ohio

Join the G-E Circle. A special program for women every week day at noon (except Saturday). On Sunday at 5:30 P. M. a program for the whole family. (Eastern Standard Time). N. B. C. coast to coast network.

GENERAL ELECTRIC
ALL-STEEL REFRIGERATOR

DOMESTIC, APARTMENT HOUSE AND COMMERCIAL REFRIGERATORS, ELECTRIC WATER COOLERS

May 1932 Good Housekeeping

A 1932 G.E. advertisement showing a pedal car (Courtesy John Rastall)

"I'm driving in for Dole," said
the wise young man,
"And make mine a BIG glass,
as fast as you can."

"It's a pure fruit juice," the
grocer did reply,
"You can't find a better drink,
however hard you try."

DRIVE IN
FOR DOLE

DOLE PINEAPPLE
JUICE
FROM HAWAII

A Steelcraft Super Charger is featured in a 1937 ad for Dole pineapple juice

drawing or require the entrant to guess the number of jelly beans or marbles in a large glass container.

Advertising wasn't the only area in which pedal cars were used to influence the behavior of the public. Children's safety and driver's training were introduced at an early age to many boys and girls across the country. It was not unusual to use pedal cars to teach youngsters the rules of the road and the way to cross the street safely. A simulated street would be set up complete with crosswalks, stoplights, and pedal car traffic.

Today America is still fascinated with the pedal car, especially as a collectors' item. Collectors and restorers want to find out all they can about pedal cars and the companies that manufactured them. In Chapter 3, a brief history of pedal car manufacturers is outlined.

Children's safety was taught to kids using pedal cars. Shown is a program being conducted in Phoenix, Arizona, during the 1950s. The pedal cars are English-made Austin J40s. (Courtesy John Rastall)

MORE

You can't measure it by slide-rule or calipers—but you'll know in your heart that the matchless thrill you get from a Lincoln-Zephyr is what you've always wanted in a motor car!

For you need only glimpse the breath-taking beauty of a Lincoln-Zephyr—feel the live horsepower of its 12 eager cylinders—relax in the cradled comfort of its magic *glider-ride*, to realize why owners everywhere get more fun per gallon in this "only-car-of-its-kind".

And that's just as true, whether you drive a Lincoln-Zephyr for business and social rounds of the town, or to make the whole sports map of America, from

Northern p

Created by standards in new Lincoln and through ent in design in engine—

Un boo you. Sound roar. Doors models are electrically operated. The famous new

Lincoln-Custom, Sedan and Limousine.

LINCOLN
Zephyr V-12

THE PEDAL CAR: MIRROR OF AUTOMOTIVE STYLING FOR THE TWENTIETH CENTURY

Throughout history, children's toys have been scaled-down creations of things that adults actually used. When the automobile made its appearance, the pedal car was soon to follow. As the automobile was invented and underwent transformations through the decades, so the pedal car was born and evolved as such that it may be described as a mirror of automotive styling for the twentieth century.

When did the first pedal car appear and who made it? This has often been the topic of discussion among serious pedal car collectors and restorers. To answer the question one must first consider that pedal cars were created in the image of real cars, but since they were toys, other inventions played a role in their creation as well. These early forerunners to the pedal car included the velocipede, the bicycle, the wagon, and the toy carriage.

The velocipede was popular in the late 1800s and came in a variety of styles. Essentially, a velocipede was a two- or three-wheeled bicycle that could be pedaled by straddling the frame. Deeply rooted in the design theory of the velocipede was that it was very efficient for a man to use his legs to propel the machine. In order for the velocipede to function, a pair of pedals and connecting rods were mated to an axle and a drive wheel, and this idea of using wheels and pedals would play a major role in the development of the pedal car.

Wagons and carriages had been around for a long time prior to the nineteenth century and were popular in the form of children's toys. With its boxy storage area and four wheels, the wagon was designed to carry loads in a stable manner. The stability that four wheels provided would prove to be a design feature that real cars as well as pedal cars would draw upon.

The handcar or "Irish Mail" was an important design development that played a role in the rise of the popularity of the pedal car. Though not a true pedal car, the handcar boasted both the ability of being self-propelled and the stability that four wheels could provide.

Opposite: First produced in 1936, the Lincoln Zephyr had a V-12 engine. Shown is a 1941 model.

Opposite, inset: Steelcraft produced a model of the Lincoln Zephyr that closely resembled the real car. This particular pedal car was restored by Larry Tynew. (Courtesy John Rastall)

A child's velocipede from the 1870s (Courtesy Henry Ford Museum)

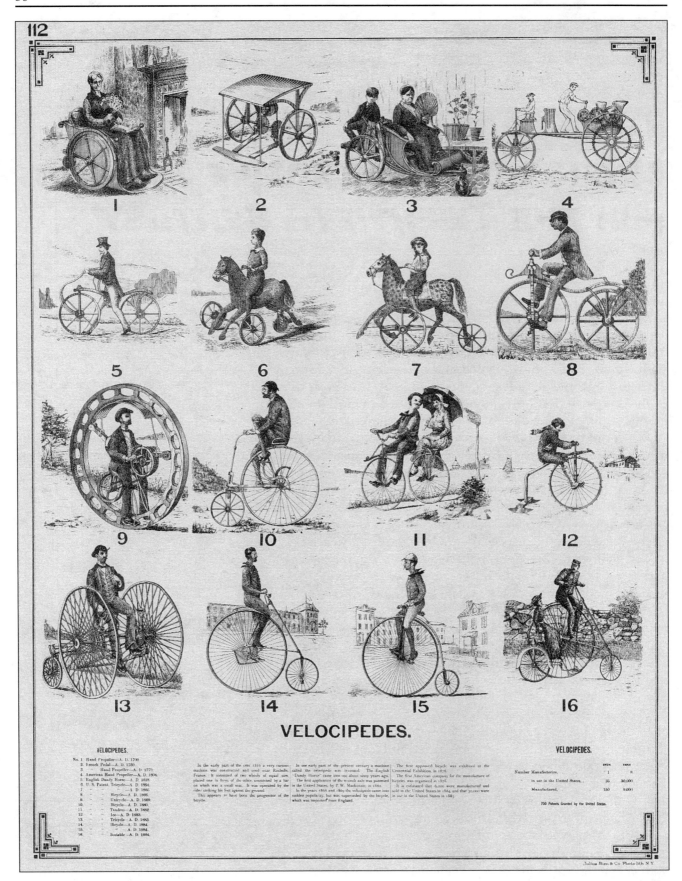

VELOCIPEDES.

Velocipedes (Courtesy John Rastall)

The pedal car had the best of all worlds. It was self-propelled by pedaling with the big muscles of the legs. It had wheels—not two or three, but the stability of four. Most importantly, the design allowed for the body to surround the driver, much like a carriage. As time went on, the body took on a variety of styles with all the flair and grace that was present in a full-size automobile.

My theory is that the first pedal car was certainly homemade and appeared during the early 1890s. Unfortunately, it is difficult to pinpoint the first prototype. (Not surprisingly, the same holds true for the automobile, as several individuals were experimenting with engines mated to a wheeled platform or buggy during the same time period.) It is known that a collector in the Midwest owns a pedal car with an early 1890s patent date. This particular toy was made by a cabinet shop in the eastern United States and may very well be the oldest surviving commercially produced pedal car.

In 1893 when the Duryea brothers built the first marketable gasoline-engine vehicle, several companies were producing tricycles, wagons, carriages, and other primitive wheeled toys. These companies included Gendron (founded in 1871) and Garton (founded in 1879).

*A turn-of-the-century buggy
(Courtesy Henry Ford Museum)*

THE PEDAL CAR: MIRROR OF AUTOMOTIVE STYLING FOR THE TWENTIETH CENTURY

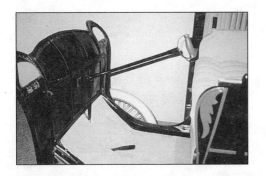

This pedal car from a 1901 catalog was sold by the Toledo Metal Wheel Company. Note the tiller steering and chain drive. (Courtesy John Rastall)

Tiller steering was used on turn-of-the-century automobiles such as this 1900 Autocar (Courtesy Henry Ford Museum)

Many cars of the early 1900s were started with hand cranks and had wooden spoked wheels (Courtesy Henry Ford Museum)

The first pedal car was probably made in the likeness of an early automobile and its design was influenced by the velocipede, the wagon, and the toy carriage. Prior to the 1890s, wheel goods catalogs showed velocipedes, bicycles, tricycles, scooters, wagons, and carriages. No pedal cars can be found, which supports the theory that the pedal car evolved along with the invention of the automobile.

During the late 1890s the automobile was referred to as a horseless carriage. More aptly it was a self-propelled buggy. This was an experimental time in the development of the automobile and various methods were used to provide power to the wheels. Steam-propelled and electric-powered vehicles were promoted; however, it was the internal combustion gasoline engine that proved most efficient and practical for the public.

Early vehicles were named after the pioneers that invented them, such as Maxim, Winton, Packard, and Olds. Autos of this era resembled open buggies and had large spoked wheels, tiller steering, carriage lamps, and various control levers. Early pedal cars that resembled the real cars of the time began to appear.

By the early 1900s, both automobiles and pedal cars had taken a foothold with the American public. Early 1900s pedal cars had sheet steel bodies and used wood for the frame and much of the floor. Large spoked wheels with solid rubber tires were the order of the day. Pedal cars were equipped like real cars, having rachet starting cranks, hanging carriage lamps, and license tags. Some pedal cars had leather, velvet, or horsehair upholstery. These toys were crudely made and weighed approximately thirty-five pounds on average. Hand stenciling of a name such as "Hummer" or "Winton" was widely used, as was gold striping to adorn the car. It wasn't unusual for the paint to be applied by a brush, along with a top coat of varnish to protect the finish. Popular colors of the day for pedal cars included, black, vermilion, green, royal blue, French gray, yellow, and white.

The 1904 Packard Model L Touring Car (Courtesy Henry Ford Museum)

The curved dash Oldsmobile

Although automobile manufacturers were trying to concentrate on reliability, styling was already creeping into the concerns of the designers. For example, the 1900 Locomobile and the curved dash Oldsmobile had crisp lines and bodies that enclosed unsightly machinery. As the early 1900s progressed, other design changes occurred. Tiller steering was becoming obsolete as steering wheels were now being installed

Henry Ford's Model T

Tin Lizzie by Garton

on many automobiles. The trend toward front engines caused manufacturers to develop unique radiator and hood shapes in order to set their cars apart from the competition. This was the age of the touring car—a time when folks could begin to explore the countryside or bring the whole family along on an extended sightseeing trip in their automobile. Packard produced a beautiful touring car that was recognizable by its distinctive radiator. Around 1906, acetylene lighting became available, which improved visibility for night travel.

In 1908, Henry Ford unveiled the Model T. The "Tin Lizzie" became the most famous car ever produced, partly because it was the first affordable "car for the great multitude." Over fifteen million Model Ts rolled off the Ford assembly line between 1908 and 1927. Decades later, many a grandfather would reminisce about this car to his grandchildren. Aware of this, the Garton Toy Company produced a "Tin Lizzie" pedal car that was available during the mid-1960s. Garton's Tin Lizzie was thirty-four inches long and came complete with simulated motor meter, headlights, and running board.

Soon after the introduction of the Model T, mass production and standardization of parts took hold in the automotive industry. By 1912 other important changes occurred, including the use of electric lights instead of lamps and electric starters in lieu of hand cranks. In 1915 Cadillac introduced the V-8 engine and the trend toward multicylinder engines was on the rise. Pedal car manufacturers were starting a trend of their own by offering pedal cars that resembled the real cars of the era. Buick, Cadillac, Packard, Pierce Arrow, Pope, and Winton were a few of the makes that pedal car manufacturers could offer the public in children-size vehicles.

The 1920s defined a glamorous era for the motorcar and ushered in the closed car that could be driven year round. As the 1920s progressed, the public could buy cars with clever options that emphasized a touch of class. A trunk or lighter could give a car that extra appeal to the buyer. The popularity of the roadster was on the rise and it was being associated with the country club crowd. Typically built as a two-seater with an emphasis on performance, many roadsters were ordered with an optional rumble seat.

During the mid-1920s pedal car manufacturers offered many kinds of roadsters. Never before could pedal cars be found in such a variety of styles and with so many options. Large fenders were in vogue, as were polished radiators and radiator ornaments. Smooth wheels with roller bearings, cantilever springs, and balloon tires helped propel some pedal cars with greater ease. Most cars had a windshield and some models featured working windshield wipers. Rumble seats, running boards, scuff plates, step plates, and bumpers could be found on many models. Just like the real thing, many pedal cars now had brake levers, shift levers, throttle and spark controls, and wooden, steel, or composition steering wheels. Horns, mirrors, and a spare tire were popular options. Other clever touches might have included a miniature oil can with bracket, a tool box and tools, a stop and slow signal, a spotlight, a luggage carrier, a motor hummer, and a detailed instrument panel. These cars were relatively heavy with an average weight of ninety-five pounds for a heavily optioned model. Preferred colors of the time included black, maroon, red, blue, yellow, dark brown, green, beige, and gray. Popular with pedal car manufacturers during the 1920s were the following makes of automobiles: Buick, Cadillac, Chevrolet, Cole, Columbia, Dodge, Durant, Essex, Ford, Haynes, Hudson, King, Marmon, Moon, Paige, Peerless, Reo, Rolls Royce, Stutz, Willys-Knight, and Winton.

One cannot discuss automobiles of the 1920s without mentioning the first car built by a major company in which styling was the main design goal. This car was the 1927 LaSalle, with a body styled by Harley J. Earl. The introduction of the LaSalle caused a sensation in the automotive world, and due to its success, General Motors created the Art and Color Sec-

THE PEDAL CAR: MIRROR OF AUTOMOTIVE STYLING FOR THE TWENTIETH CENTURY

A popular option on a 1920s roadster was the rumble seat, such as this one on a 1927 LaSalle (Courtesy Henry Ford Museum)

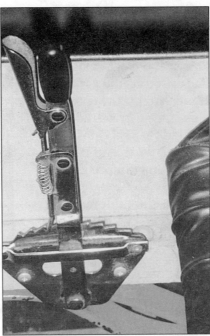
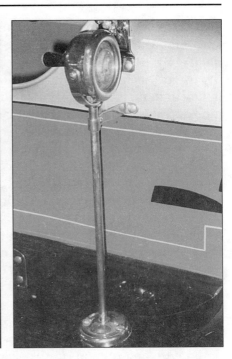

Details like a miniature oil can, a shift lever, and a spotlight were clever touches added to pedal cars of the 1920s and 1930s

Louvered hoods and disc wheels were in vogue during the early 1920s as seen on this 1926 Wills Sainte Claire (Courtesy Henry Ford Museum)

American Motorist, *August, 1927*

...c'est l'affaire faite...

ADDING WOMEN'S FAVOR TO MEN'S ACCLAIM

It was a foregone conclusion that the LaSalle would fire the enthusiasm of men who admire dashing performance. Probably never before, however, has any car made so complete a conquest of men and women alike.

The La Salle is distinctly and emphatically a man's car by virtue of the red-blooded virility it displays in every requirement or emergency a motor car can meet. But it is also just as emphatically a woman's car—not merely because it is the observed of observers, by reason of its rare and exquisite beauty—but because it handles and obeys a woman's touch with a sureness, an ease and a delicacy that delights the feminine love of lightness and grace.

You may possess a LaSalle on the liberal term-payment plan of the General Motors Acceptance Corporation—the famous G.M.A.C. plan

CADILLAC MOTOR CAR COMPANY
DIVISION OF GENERAL MOTORS CORPORATION

DETROIT, MICHIGAN   OSHAWA, CANADA

LA SALLE

From $2495 to $2685, f. o. b. Detroit

MANUFACTURED · COMPLETELY · BY · THE · CADILLAC · MOTOR · CAR · COMPANY · WITHIN · ITS · OWN · PLANTS

The 1927 LaSalle marked the beginning of true automotive styling. Made by the Cadillac Motor Car Company, the LaSalle featured a 303 C.I.D. V-8 engine and had a base price of $2495.

Luxury cars of the early 1930s, such as this 1930 Auburn, featured wire spoked wheels and balloon tires (Courtesy Henry Ford Museum)

Rear fender detail on a full-size 1934 DeSoto Airflow (Courtesy Henry Ford Museum)

1936 DeSoto Airflow pedal car owned by Bruce Beimers (Courtesy John Rastall)

tion. For the first time, GM had full-time design specialists working on the appearance of future automobiles. From then on, cars were more than just machines—they were made with style and personality. By 1929 automobiles were selling in record numbers; however, economic storm clouds were gathering on the horizon. The stock market crash and the ensuing Depression put a damper on car sales and devastated small independent manufacturers.

The Great Depression of the 1930s closed the pocketbooks of the American people, but not the creative minds of the automotive designers. The decade began with cars being designed with a lower profile, but in a few years aerodynamic bodies started a trend toward streamlining. Thus emerged the most radical and influential design of the 1930s, the 1934 Chrysler Airflow and DeSoto Airflow. The Airflow not only looked different, it was different. Besides being streamlined, the car had improved weight distribution, more interior room, and increased structural strength over previous models. Unfortunately, overall sales were poor, as the majority of the car-buying public thought the car was ugly. A pedal car version of the Airflow, produced by American National, had working headlights and horn. The Airflow pedal car is very popular with collectors and could escalate in value over the next few years.

Pedal cars of the 1930s were larger and heavier than in any other period in history. Streamlining began to take hold by mid-decade with American National, Gendron, and Steelcraft all offering new designs. Artillery wheels with large plated hubcaps were featured and hood ornaments resembled graceful works of art. Many cars had bullet style headlamps and some deluxe models could be ordered with

"Come on Along . . ."

MOTORING IS FUN AGAIN!"

The New Airflow Chryslers give you thrilling new driving sensations that result from interesting scientific facts.

You get a glorious sense of freedom at high speeds because the authentic streamline design eliminates vacuum and wind drag. For the same reason, acceleration from 40 to 60 is as spirited as it is from 15 to 30.

You enjoy a Floating Ride over even the worst of roads because the new distribution of weight slows down the periodicity of the springs . . . sharp jolts are lengthened into easy glides.

You feel a magical sensation of effortless ease when the *automatic overdrive changes

gear ratios for you as you pass 40 miles an hour . . . cutting engine speed one third . . . reducing fuel consumption as much as 20% at 40 miles an hour, 25% at 60.

You can actually feel the safety you get from the Airflow Chrysler's unit body and frame. Forty times as rigid as an ordinary frame, this strong bridgework of steel not only contributes vastly to steadiness on the road but also prevents road shocks and jiggling vibrations from assaulting your nerves.

In everything it is and does, the Airflow Chrysler provides a whole new travel experience. You can easily prove it for yourself!

Four Distinguished 1934 Models

CHRYSLER AIRFLOW EIGHT . . . 122 horsepower and 123-inch wheelbase. Six-passenger Sedan, Brougham and Town Sedan, five-passenger Coupe. All body types. $1345.

CHRYSLER AIRFLOW IMPERIAL . . . 130 horsepower . . . 128-inch wheelbase. Six-passenger Sedan and Town Sedan, five-passenger Coupe. All body types. $1625.

AIRFLOW CUSTOM IMPERIAL . . . 150 horsepower . . . 146-inch wheelbase. Individualized body types, prices on request.

1934 CHRYSLER SIX . . . *With independently sprung front wheels . . . for a smooth, cushioned ride . . . 93 horsepower, 7 body types on 117-inch and 121-inch wheelbase. Priced from $775 up. Four-door Sedan, $845. *Automatic overdrive standard on Imperial and Custom Imperial. Available at slight additional cost on Airflow Eight. Duplate safety plate glass in all windows of all models at only $10 additional. List prices at factory, Detroit, subject to change without notice.

Write for the interesting free Floating Ride booklet. Chrysler Sales Corporation, 12193 East Jefferson Avenue, Detroit, Mich.

The Chrysler Airflow caused a sensation at the 1934 auto show; however, due to slow sales the model line was dropped after only four years. Interestingly, many of its concepts were later adopted by other manufacturers.

The Packard Eight Sedan for Five Passengers

What a Packard!

WE URGE you to see the new 1935 Packard.

Inspect its modern streamlining, its magnificent new interior treatment. Notice that the famous Packard identifying lines have not only been retained, but actually have been emphasized. *What a beautiful Packard!*

Then enter the car. Here's a roominess you've never known before. The widest, most comfortable seats you ever sat in. The doors are easier to get into and out of. The windshield is wider, the windows larger, giving you greater vision than ever before. *What a spacious, comfortable Packard!*

Now drive the car. Packard engineers, by increasing the tread and redistributing weight, have made the new Packard even easier to ride in and easier to handle than last year's car. *And what a brilliantly performing Packard!*

Packard engineers, by utilizing new materials and redesigning parts, have also produced the toughest, longest-lived car in Packard's history. They have created a motor so perfect that, were the equator a road, you could drive the car half-way around the world *in a week* without harming the motor

in any way. *What a rugged Packard!*

We repeat the invitation: See and drive this new car. After that, we believe you will soon be driving one of your own, while people exclaim as you pass: *"What a Packard!"*

ON THE AIR: *Packard presents LAWRENCE TIBBETT, John B. Kennedy and a distinguished orchestra every Tuesday evening, 8:30 to 9:15 E.S.T., W.J.Z. Network, N.B.C.*

PACKARD

ASK THE MAN WHO OWNS ONE

Big cars like this 1935 Packard were in style for the 1930s. Relying on its solid reputation, the company urged those interested in buying a Packard to "Ask the man who owns one."

"But officer—when I told you I was just going to get a hat pretty enough for my new Ford, you said yourself THAT wouldn't be easy!"

DISTINCTIVE BEAUTY BORN OF USEFULNESS

Ford V·8

FOR 1937

TODAY's world wants beauty born of usefulness . . . form that follows function . . . lines both pleasing and practical.

By such modern standards, the 1937 Ford V-8 is unmistakably beautiful. It's wide, low, roomy. No horns, headlamps or spare tires break its smooth, clean curves. Every detail, inside and out, contributes to its simple, distinguished design.

There's beauty of another kind in its fine materials, precision workmanship, faithful service. And there's beauty in its budget figures too!

Both the improved 85-horsepower V-8 engine and the new 60-horsepower V-8 engine provide smooth performance with economy. In fact, the "60" engine, optional in five standard body types, makes possible the lowest Ford price in years and the greatest gas mileage ever built into a Ford car.

The 1937 Ford reflected the trend toward streamlining

THE PEDAL CAR: MIRROR OF AUTOMOTIVE STYLING FOR THE TWENTIETH CENTURY

Pondering deep thoughts is Count Alexis de Sakhnoffsky. A premier engineering stylist of the 1930s, the "Count" was known for his streamlined designs of automobiles, refrigerators, clocks, office furniture, bicycles, and pedal cars. One of his most stylish creations was the Streamliner, which made its debut in 1937 and was manufactured by Steelcraft.
(Courtesy John Rastall)

electric lights and horns. The Steelcraft Streamliner was new for 1937 and featured a one-piece body of stamped steel. Several pedal cars popular with collectors and restorers exist from this era, including the Lincoln Tandem by American National, the Steelcraft Streamliner, and the Gendron Skippy Roadster to name a few.

During World War II, America concentrated on producing tanks, planes, jeeps, and other war machines. Pedal car manufacturers also offered their versions of military vehicles. For example, Garton produced a U.S. Army Tank Division Scout Car complete with turret and antitank gun. Pedal jeeps became popular after the war and many were offered through the 1950s.

As far as real cars were concerned, postwar vehicles such as the 1946 Frazer and 1948 Hudson had a heavy, almost swollen appearance. Very interesting was the 1948 Tucker with its rear engine and its "cyclops eye" headlight. This headlight would follow the direction that the steering wheel was being turned. Only fifty-three Tuckers were built, making these vehicles extremely collectible today. Another unusual car was the three-wheeled Davis. Made between 1947 and 1949, only seventeen were ever produced. "Looking fine for 49" was the Buick Roadmaster with its massive gracefulness and four portholes in each front fender. Murray Ohio offered a pedal car version named the Torpedo. Collectors refer to this pedal car as a "Porthole Buick."

Many other notable pedal cars were produced and sold during the 1940s. Garton offered a Mercury station wagon with wood paneling, also known as a "Woody." Gendron offered a version of its Skippy Roadster with an opening hood complete with simulated engine. Steelcraft made a version of a 1941 Chrysler that is very popular with restorers today. Postwar pedal cars have fewer options and less detailing than earlier models. Even the top of the line 1940s models couldn't quite match the craftsmanship of the deluxe pedal cars of the late 1920s and early 1930s.

The 1950s found designers trying to create fantasy cars that had jet plane and spaceship themes. General Motors produced a number of dream cars during this era and introduced the Corvette in 1953. Besides production cars, another type of vehicle became popular during this time period. These vehicles were known as hot rods. A typical hot rod had a souped-up V-8 engine and a Model T roadster body. Owners of these hot rods enjoyed cruising up and down the boulevard or engaging in drag races.

Pedal car offerings reflected the styling trends of the '50s. Garton produced the Kidillac, which highly resembled the 1950 Cadillac. Other popular Garton products were the Hot Rod and the Space Cruiser, which were new for 1953. Murray Ohio had a large array of pedal vehicles available during this era, including the Atomic Missile airplane, the Good Humor cycle, the Fire Truck, the Ranch Wagon, the Comet, and the Champion.

The 1949 Buick Roadmaster Convertible Sedan had four distinctive portholes in each front fender. Push button controls operated the power top, the front seat, and the windows.

In 1950 Murray produced a pedal car known as the Torpedo, styled after the 1949 Buick Roadmaster

The 1941 Chrysler Convertible

A 1941 Chrysler pedal car by Steelcraft
(Courtesy John Rastall)

The 1941 Pontiac was very affordable with a base price of $828

1941 Pontiac pedal car by Steelcraft (Courtesy John Rastall)

White sidewall tires at extra cost, when available

The 1947 Mercury Wagon, also called a "Woody,"
had a base price of $1676

Complete with wood paneling was the Garton
Mercury Wagon (Courtesy John Rastall)

Touting "First by far with a postwar car!" was the 1947 Studebaker Champion

*During the 1950s Murray Ohio was selling
Champion pedal cars*

*Norm Wallace's Roadster epitomized the hot rod of
the late 1950s*

The Garton Hot Rod

The 1959 Ford Fairlane 500

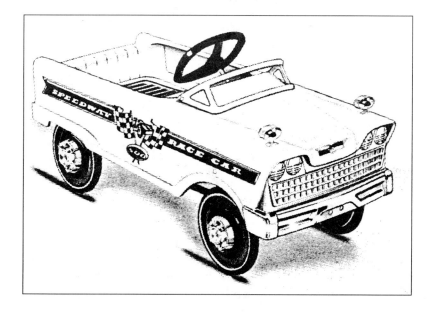

Murray Ohio produced a pedal car body styled after the '59 Ford (Courtesy John Rastall)

Above: The 1950 Cadillac Series Sixty-Two Convertible

Right: A Garton Kidillac pedal car (Courtesy John Rastall)

The typical car of the 1950s had lots of chrome like this 1955 Chevy Bel Air (Courtesy Henry Ford Museum)

Enormous fins and dual rocket taillights made the 1959 Eldorado look like it was meant to fly, not drive. Equipped with a 390 Overhead Valve V-8 engine, the Eldorado weighed in at a hefty 5,060 lbs. Styled by Harley Earl, this would be his last big project for GM. (Courtesy Henry Ford Museum)

By 1956, tailfins and hooded headlights were evident on many cars. Popular also were dual headlights and the lavish use of chrome trim. Ford's Fairlane 500 for 1959 had all these features and was awarded a gold medal at the Brussels World Fair. Murray Ohio created a steel stamping that was patterned after this body style. By adding different paint schemes, options, and graphics, this body style could be any number of different models for Murray. No car could sum up the late 1950's excessive use of ornamentation better than the 1959 Cadillac Eldorado. This car featured a highly detailed, chrome-laden grille and enormous tail fins with rocket shaped lenses. Big outrageous cars wouldn't last, as the country was experiencing a recession. This meant sales of foreign compacts like the Volkswagen were on the rise.

The early 1960s saw the introduction of several domestic compact cars such as the AMC Rambler, the Dodge Lancer, and the Ford Falcon; however, the big success story is reserved for the Ford Mustang. Introduced in April of 1964, the Mustang was unique, sporty, somewhat practical, and most importantly, cheap. The public loved this new pony car and bought over a half a million during 1965. This made Mustang the most successful new car ever introduced in America. Coinciding with the release of the Ford Mustang was the introduction of the AMF Mustang pedal car. The pedal car version looked re-

In some instances an automotive manufacturer would authorize or sanction the production of a new model of pedal car to coincide with the launch of a new model of full-size automobile. The Mustang pedal car by AMF was available by Christmas of 1965 and rode a wave of popularity for many years, as did the first generation of Mustang by Ford Motor Company. (Courtesy John Rastall)

INTRODUCING THE DEPENDABLES FOR '64

We didn't invent the compact . . .

we just enlarged upon it!

The original idea about compacts has little similarity to the 1964 Dart idea. Now don't get us wrong. Dart certainly is a compact. It parks almost anywhere. It steers quickly, handles lightly. It's about as easy on gas as you hope to get. But from there on out the old idea and the new part company . . . Because Dart's the compact in the large economy size! Dart looks bigger. It sits bigger.

It's powered bigger. And the Dart trunk is actually larger than many standard-size cars. When you add it all up, here's a lot of car going for you. A lot of room and comfort. A lot of durability and service-saving features. A lot of good looks that take you out of the compact class without taking you away from a compact price. The 1964 Dodge Dart! America's new family-size favorite.

Compact Dodge Dart

DODGE DIVISION — **CHRYSLER** MOTORS CORPORATION

A switch to compact cars occurred in the early 1960s. The ad agency committed a blunder by showing a Kidillac in this Dodge Dart ad for 1964. Obviously, the Kidillac is associated with a GM product, the Cadillac.

markably like the real thing and sold for $12.95. Today, a similar style of Mustang pedal car is being reproduced—yours for only $395.00.

Seeing what was happening with the full-size Mustang, the competition began to crank out their version of the pony car. Chevy offered the Camaro, Pontiac came out with the Firebird, and Plymouth created the Barracuda. By the late '60s the emphasis was on performance and many cars could be ordered with big block engines. Muscle cars dominated the market and performance ruled until just after the 1970 model year.

Pedal cars during the 1960s emerged with decals and plastic trim and some could be ordered with a wild metallic finish. Garton produced a pedal train, the Casey Jones Locomotive, along with a complete line of pedal cars in the early 1960s. Murray and AMF also had a large array of products for the consumer to choose from.

The 1970s brought many modifications in automotive design due to new safety and emission requirements. Oil prices skyrocketed, triggering a recession. As real cars were undergoing styling changes, pedal cars were going out of style. Of the product lines that remained, most manufacturers had switched to thinner gauge metal and plastic pedals. In 1974 AMF sold a number of plastic-bodied pedal cars, including a

A Mustang ad that appeared in a magazine in June 1964

*The Casey Jones Locomotive had a smokestack,
bell, cowcatcher, and simulated headlight
(Courtesy John Rastall)*

version of the Flintstonemobile. By the late '70s, only a few styles of metal-bodied pedal cars remained. Body styles were very limited with no real car influence. One could still order a metal-bodied pedal car as late as 1985 from a distributor of AMF products.

Today's pedal cars are made of specialized plastics that are weather and damage resistant. Neon colors are popular, along with caster type wheels. The design of these toys is based upon safety and function rather than style. Interestingly, sales of these new breed of pedal cars are easily outstripping sales of full-size automobiles. This means that the pedal car can hardly be called extinct, and that a whole new generation of enthusiasts are in the making.

BENCHMARKS IN AUTOMOTIVE HISTORY

The following list of benchmarks in automotive history may aid those who wish to date their pedal car. It should be noted that particular makes or features found on full-size automobiles were not available until certain years; therefore, it is likely that these makes or features would not be found on pedal cars produced before the corresponding year of the full-size vehicle.

1895   Duryea Motor Wagon Co. formed

1896   Winton and Columbia cars are born

1897   Olds Motor Vehicles, Autocar, and Kelsey cars appear

1899   Packard, Stearns, Studebaker, Toledo, and Franklin arrive

1900   Peerless, Auburn, Knox, Garford, and Rambler are here

1902   Tiller steering began converting over to steering wheels

The H-slot shifter is patented by Packard

Buick, Cadillac, Jackson, and Marmon names appear

1903   Columbus, Maxwell, Overland, and Pope-Hartford cars arrive

1905   Kissel, Moon, and Reo are new names this year

1907   First suspension with springs over axles on runabouts

Oakland and Speedwell cars are available

1908   Paterson, Regal, Seldon, Sears, and Simplex cars are for sale

1909   Cole, Hupmobile, and Hudson appear

1911   Chevrolet, King, and Stutz are formed

1912   Hand cranks began changing over to starters

Electric lights begin to replace lamps

1913   Chandler, Republic, and Saxon are new this year

1914   First Moto-Meter appears

Spare tire on rear becomes popular

Dodge Brothers, Singer, and Willys-Knight are formed

1915   V-8 engine is introduced

1916   Dixie Flyer, Jordan, and Wolverine are newly available

A toy store's display shows the current selection of pedal powered vehicles

1919	Hood louvers become popular
1921	Ace, Durant, and Fox names appear
1923	Cole 8 is first car to have balloon tires
	Alemite chassis lube is introduced
1925	Chrysler is officially formed
1927	Styling comes of age as LaSalle and Imperial are introduced
1928	Plymouth and DeSoto are new
1929	Radios are introduced into cars
1930	Willys, Austin, and Graham are born
1932	Skirted fenders are introduced
1934	Streamlining gains attention with the Chrysler Airflow
1937	Lincoln Zephyr can top 90 mph
1938	Gear shift lever introduced to steering column

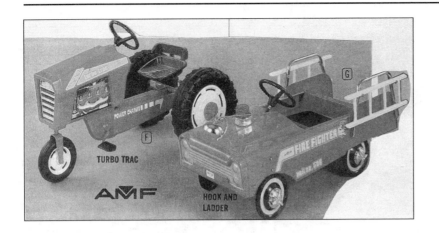

Examples of two pedal toys that AMF sold in the late 1970s

1941   Pontiac's Custom Torpedo 8 is best selling, mid-priced car

1943   Command cars, tanks, and jeeps are built for war effort

1953   Corvette is introduced

1956   Tailfins and hooded headlights are popular

1957   Most cars have big fins, lots of chrome, and dual headlights

1959   Cadillac has giant fins, large chrome grille, and rocket taillights

1961   Compact models AMC Rambler and Dodge Lancer introduced

1965   Ford Mustang is best selling new "pony car"

1967   Chevrolet introduces the Camaro

1969   Muscle cars dominate the market

Pontiac GTO and Plymouth GTX are performance-oriented

1970   Ford Maverick is introduced as muscle cars yield to economical models

(List adapted from *100 Years of Automotive History* by John Gunnell, courtesy of the author)

This customized 1950s Murray Torpedo sold for $3,220 at a Christie's New York auction. An attractive pedal car at auction can bring unpredictable prices. (Courtesy Christie's New York, New York)

PEDAL CAR PRICE GUIDE

A NOTE REGARDING PRICES

The prices listed in this book are not fixed values and should serve the collector as a guide only. Prices are based on data gathered from collectors, auction results, pedal car shows, and classified advertisements. This information reflects current trends of buying and selling in the pedal car market. The collector should be aware that deluxe, original pedal cars that are well-preserved may be bid to unpredictably high prices at auction. Concerning restored pedal cars, the quality of the restoration will impact the final selling price; therefore, neither the author nor the publisher can be held responsible for gains or losses from using this price guide.

When using this price guide, keep these points in mind: A well-preserved pedal car will have the original paint, showing only minor scuffs, scratches, and oxidation. The car must be complete, with all parts and trim intact. A restored pedal car refers to a pedal car that has undergone a complete restoration and should reflect quality workmanship. An inferior restoration will reduce the value of the pedal car. Poorly preserved originals may be worth considerably less than the values quoted. Regional variations may cause these prices to be higher or lower in some areas of the United States.

PEDAL CAR PRICE GUIDE

Make	Model	Year	Well-Preserved Original	Restored
Amer. Nat'l	Cadillac	1920	$5000	$2500
Amer. Nat'l	Paige	1925	6000	4500
Amer. Nat'l	Airflow	1935	10,000	6500
Amer. Nat'l	Air Pilot	1935	6500	4000
Amer. Nat'l	Buick	1935	7000	5500
Amer. Nat'l	Cadillac	1935	7500	5700
Amer. Nat'l	Fire Chief	1935	5500	3500
Amer. Nat'l	Fire Tower	1935	7500	4500
Amer. Nat'l	Hose Auto	1935	7000	4000
Amer. Nat'l	LaSalle	1935	7500	5700
Amer. Nat'l	Lincoln Roadster	1935	15,000	10,000
Amer. Nat'l	Packard	1935	7000	5500
Amer. Nat'l	Nash	1935	7000	5500
Amer. Nat'l	Racer	1935	5500	4000
Amer. Nat'l	Tandem	1935	10,000	6500
Amer. Nat'l	Wasp	1935	4000	2500
Amer. Nat'l	White Truck	1935	4500	3000
AMF	Cab-Over Truck	1959	1000	800
AMF	Mustang	1965	900	700
AMF	Dragster	1966	300	200
AMF	Jet Sweep	1966	400	300
AMF	GTO	1969	400	300
AMF	GTX	1969	400	300
AMF	Fire Chief 512	1969	400	300
AMF	Fire Pumper 519	1969	450	350
AMF	Probe 3	1969	400	300
AMF	Probe Jr.	1969	300	200
AMF	F.F. 503	1980	200	150
AMF	F.F. 508	1980	250	175

Mid-1970s AMF Fire Fighter 508

Make	Model	Year	Well-Preserved Original	Restored
BMC	Dump Truck	1954	800	600
BMC	Hook & Ladder	1954	800	600
BMC	Jetliner	1954	900	700
BMC	Racer	1954	1100	900
BMC	Station Wagon	1954	800	600
BMC	Thunderbolt	1954	800	600
BMC	Tractor Jr.	1954	200	150
Eska	Oliver 88	1947	2000	1500
Eska	Allis Chalmers C	1949	1200	850
Eska	Farmall H	1949	1200	850
Graphic Repr.	Ford 900	1954	3000	2000
Eska	John Deere 60	1955	1000	800
Eska	Case-O-Matic	1958	1000	750
Eska	John Deere 130	1958	900	700
Garton	Hummer	1916	2500	1500
Garton	Tractor	1916	1500	1000
Garton	Winton	1916	3500	2000
Garton	Buick	1938	5000	3500
Garton	Ford	1938	5000	3500
Garton	LaSalle	1938	5000	3500
Garton	Lincoln	1938	5500	4000
Garton	Pontiac	1938	5000	3500
Garton	Army Car	1941	2500	1800
Garton	Divebomber	1941	3000	2000
Garton	Station Wagon	1941	2000	1500
Garton	Space Cruiser	1953	1500	900
Garton	Police	1955	1000	800
Garton	Fire Truck	1957	800	600
Garton	Hot Rod	1957	1500	1000
Garton	Kidillac	1957	2000	1500
Garton	Ranch Wagon	1957	800	600
Garton	Mark 5	1959	800	600
Garton	Casey Jones	1961	900	700
Garton	Tin Lizzy	1961	600	450

Early 1960s Garton Tin Lizzie (missing hood ornament, windshield, and horn)

PEDAL CAR PRICE GUIDE

Make	Model	Year	Well-Preserved Original	Restored
Gendron	Locomotive	1916	4500	2500
Gendron	Race Car	1924	4000	3000
Gendron	Jordan	1927	7000	4000
Gendron	Aeroplane	1938	7000	4000
Gendron	Hose Cart	1938	7000	4000
Gendron	Marmon	1938	8000	5000
Gendron	Packard	1938	10,000	6500
Gendron	Pierce Arrow	1938	8000	5000
Gendron	Speed Boat	1938	5500	3000
Gendron	Skippy Roadster	1939	3500	2000
Hamilton	Jeep	1958	600	450
Kirk-Latty	Cadillac	1914	3500	1500
Midwest	Jet Hawk	1959	900	750
Murray	Champion	1950	900	750
Murray	Pontiac	1950	1000	800
Murray	Buick Torpedo	1954	2500	1800
Murray	Comet	1954	2000	1500
Murray	Dump Truck	1954	1200	800
Murray	Fire Truck	1954	900	750
Murray	Station Wagon	1954	900	750
Murray	Super Sonic Jet	1954	1500	1000
Murray	Good Humor	1956	1500	900
Murray	Atomic Missile	1958	1000	800
Murray	Speedway Pace	1961	600	400
Murray	Super Tot Rod	1961	300	250
Murray	Tee Bird	1961	450	375
Murray	Fireball Racer	1963	450	375
Murray	Dolphin	1968	900	700
Murray	Jolly Roger	1968	900	700
New London Metal Processing	D-4 Caterpillar	1949	3500	2500
Steelcraft	Cadillac	1924	4000	3000
Steelcraft	Buick Roadster	1928	6500	4000
Steelcraft	Mack Truck	1929	4000	3000
Steelcraft	Packard	1932	7500	4500
Steelcraft	Chrysler	1933	7500	4500
Steelcraft	Airflow	1936	6500	4000
Steelcraft	Airflow Fire	1936	4500	3500
Steelcraft	Streamliner	1937	4500	3500
Steelcraft	Supercharger	1937	5000	4000

Make	Model	Year	Well-Preserved Original	Restored
Steelcraft	Lincoln Zephyr	1939	4000	3000
Steelcraft	Buick	1941	3500	2500
Steelcraft	Chrysler	1941	3000	2000
Steelcraft	Pontiac	1941	3000	2000
Steelcraft	Pursuit Plane	1941	3500	2500
Steelcraft	Spitfire	1941	3500	2500

1941 Steelcraft Supercharger Deluxe

Auction Action in Sandwich, Mass.

Passed by Cape Dealers, Pedal Truck brings $77,000

SANDWICH, MASS. — A 1928 American National pedal fire truck was bid to $70,000 plus premium at Sandwich Auction House on Wednesday, July 12. A retired salesman for H.P. Hood Dairy, James Custodio, and his wife Claire consigned the toy to auction after several Cape Cod dealers refused to pay even $150 for the collectible.

Auctioneer Russell Johnson said that the Toledo made pedal truck sold to a Western Massachusetts man underbid by an Albany buyer.

"It is our belief and understanding that it is going to a collector on the West Coast," Sandwich Auction House president Donald

Gray said. Mr Gray added that both the bidder and the underbidder first learned of the approaching sale from *Antiques and The Arts Weekly.*

In excellent condition, the 5'11" vehicle is thought to be about one of 500 examples outfitted with such deluxe features as ladders, a spotlight, running board, tool box and windshield.

Mr Johnson said that the fire truck was the best he had ever seen. He initially thought it might sell for as much as $2,000, but the delirious response of antique toy collectors prompted him to put the estimate at a daring $2,8/3,200.

About 300 attended the standing-room-only sale. The auctioneer opened bidding at $8,000. Bidding proceeded at $5,000 increments.

Mrs Custodio inherited the truck from a cousin, a priest who died about 25 years ago. The toy was stored until a recent housecleaning. A similar pedal fire engine reportedly sold for about $34,000 five years ago.

Mr Gray said that the fire truck was the single largest sale for Sandwich Auction House since its opening in 1974.

—LAURA BEACH

At present, this 1928 pedal fire truck holds the record for highest price paid for a pedal car at auction.

1941 Steelcraft Pursuit Plane

RESTORED AND ORIGINAL CONDITION PEDAL CARS

Restored Pedal Cars

1933 Chrysler Roadster by Steelcraft*

Left, from the top:
1929 Stutz Roadster by Steelcraft*

1926 Dodge Roadster by American National*

Below: 1928 Packard Rumble Seat Roadster
by Gendron*

1928 Lincoln by Gendron*

Right: 1924 Fire Pumper No. 6 by Toledo*

1935 White Dump Truck by American National*

Right: 1932 Spirit of St. Louis by American National*

1925 Federal Dump Truck by Toledo*

Right: 1932 Sunbeam Racer No. 8 by Gendron*

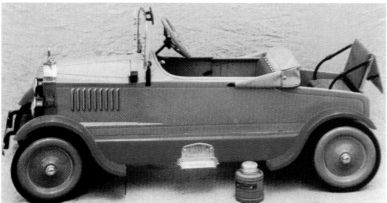

*Above: 1928 National by American National**

*Left top: : 1929 Mack Dump Truck by Steelcraft**

*Left bottom: 1935 Hose Reeled Fire Truck by American National**

*Left: 1927 Buick Rumble Seat Roadster by American National**

*Below: 1928 Buick Five-Wheeled Roadster by Steelcraft**
* These photos courtesy of Noel Barrett Antiques and Auctions Ltd.

1941 Custom Buick Police Car by Steelcraft

Right: 1949 D-4 Caterpillar by New London Metal Processing

1935 G-Man Cruiser by Toledo

1926 Packard by American National

Right: 1941 Streamliner by Steelcraft, owned by Boy Toys

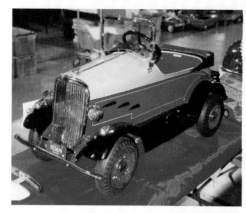

Above: 1934 Hupmobile by Steelcraft, owned by Boy Toys

Left top: 1937 Skippy DeSoto Airflow by American National, owned by Boy Toys

Left: 1938 Hudson 8 by Gendron

Below: 1958 Custom Atomic Missile by Murray Ohio (restored by Dan Smith and John Byers)

1935 Chrysler Airflow by Gendron, owned by Boy Toys

Right: 1958 John Deere 130 by Eska (restored by the author)

1941 Pontiac by Murray Ohio

Right: 1967 Jolly Roger by Murray Ohio

1955 Good Humor Truck by Murray Ohio

Right: 1953 Special Racer by BMC

Original Condition Pedal Cars

1925 Paige by American National*

Left: 1930 Water Tower Fire Truck by American National*

Left: 1924 Race Car No. 6 by Gendron*

Below: 1933 Buick Roadster by Toledo*

1924 Red Bird Roadster by American National*

Right: A typical pedal car from the early 1900s, maker unknown (owned by J. Rastall)

Right: 1927 Jordan Roadster by Gendron*

Below: 1983 Fire Fighter 508 by AMF-Roadmaster

From the Top:
1963 Atomic Missile by Murray Ohio

1920 Cadillac by American National*

1954 Fire Truck by Murray Ohio

* These photos courtesy of Noel Barrett Antiques
and Auctions Ltd.

PEDAL CAR RESTORATIONS:

Before and After

D-4 Caterpillar by New London Metal Processing, owned by Van Eden

Champion by Murray Ohio, restored by Mel Davis

AMF 508 Hook & Ladder, restored by Dave Harrington

Murray Ranger, restored by D. Harrington

1941 Chrysler by Steelcraft, restored by Jeff Balog

Garton tractor, owned by Van Eden

Buick Torpedo by Murray Ohio, restored by the author

Jet Hawk Sportster by Midwest Industries, restored by Robert G. Hann

1941 Pontiac Automobile by Steelcraft, restored by Dave Harrington

Hook & Ladder by Midwest Industries, restored by Dave Harrington

BMC Blue Streak, restored by Dave Harrington

Murray Ohio Pursuit Plane, owned by Van Eden

Pontiac Station Wagon by Murray Ohio, restored by Jeff Balog

Dump truck by Murray Ohio, restored by D. Harrington

Murray Fireball Racer, restored by D. Harrington

WHEEL GOODS ART AND ADVERTISING

Not all children were fortunate enough to own a pedal car, so it was not unusual to make a home-made car out of an old garbage can, as shown in this 1960 lithograph entitled "Watch Out Grandpa" (Courtesy John Rastall)

Below: Children's cars were sometimes used in advertising to sell full-size automobiles. This ad, which features an electric powered children's vehicle, appeared in Sports Illustrated *in June of 1959. (Courtesy John Rastall)*

One of the giant companies that produced wheel goods was Murray Ohio. Shown is the cover of their 1965 catalog.

CHAPTER 3

A CONDENSED HISTORY OF AMERICAN PEDAL CAR MANUFACTURERS

Anyone who has ever owned a pedal car may be naturally curious about pedal car manufacturers. One may wonder exactly when a certain company was in operation, how it got started, and why it is not making pedal cars today. Over the years, collectors have attempted to gather information on old pedal car companies, but the information is very scarce and has led many enthusiasts to rely on conjecture and rumors to explain the history of various pedal car manufacturers.

Through library research, fellow enthusiasts, original catalogs, advertising, photographs, and personal interviews with former pedal car company employees, I have attempted to gather the facts about several pedal car manufacturers. It should be noted that many companies had a complex history and went through a great number of changes over the years. In addition, an unknown number of pedal car companies were in operation for a short period of time and then went out of business or merged with other companies. This was not so unusual, as many automobile companies in the early part of the century also struggled to find their niche in the automotive market. Some pedal car companies were in business for a long time and made large profits; others failed and had to close their doors after only a few years.

It is well-known that Detroit was and still is the car capital of the country. Not as well-known is that at one time, Toledo, Ohio, was the pedal car capital. Several wheel companies that would eventually begin making wheel goods were started in or around Toledo and by the 1920s many of these small companies merged to form the world's largest manufacturer of pedal cars—American National, located in Toledo, Ohio.

As time went on, pedal car companies came and went and it is interesting to examine why pedal car manufacturers decided to no longer produce children's vehicles. In many cases, companies pursued other manufacturing areas with a higher growth potential. For example, the popularity of the

A CONDENSED HISTORY OF AMERICAN PEDAL CAR MANUFACTURERS

Plastic toys, such as the Marx "Big Wheel" and the "Green Machine" helped usher out the era of the metal-bodied pedal car

lawnmower was one of the factors that led Murray to drop its pedal car manufacturing. The small profit margin on making pedal cars made the company very nervous if sales dipped. Some pedal car companies were greatly affected by the stock market crash of 1929 and could not survive the Depression years that followed. Such was the case of the Sidway-Topliff Corporation, which had been dealt a serious blow years earlier with the untimely death of Charles Sidway.

For a time during World War II, metal was directed away from the production of such things as pedal cars, and pedal car companies switched to making war machines. After the war, pedal car production resumed; however, the lavish, heavy cars of the prewar years would no longer be made. As the years marched on, the pedal car would have to compete against other manufacturing interests. By the 1960s, bicycles and lawnmowers were hot sellers, forcing companies to decide whether to pursue making a popular new product or to operate at status quo.

The increasing use of plastics contributed to the demise of the metal-bodied pedal car. Plastic was cheaper, lighter, didn't require painting, and would not rust. A good example of a plastic riding toy that helped usher out the pedal car was the Marx "Big Wheel." Plastic toys could be designed in new configurations to meet consumer product safety standards. On the other hand, the safety of the old stamped steel pedal cars was under scrutiny. It would be easier for some manufacturers such as AMF to change to plastic than to try to comply with new consumer regulations.

Like most companies, pedal car manufacturers were in business to make a profit. They were driven to various business decisions based on the behavior of the buying public. If customers were not purchasing pedal cars, then pedal car companies could not justify producing them any longer.

THE AMERICAN NATIONAL COMPANY

The American National Company was actually a conglomerate of companies that merged in the 1920s into one single organization that sold wheel goods. The merging companies consisted of the Toledo Metal Wheel Company, which was founded in 1887 by Frank Southard; the National Wheel Company located in Perrysburg, Ohio; the American Metal Wheel Company, founded by J. S. Schoenfield and John McKisson; and the Juvenile Vehicle Woodwork Company, started by F. A. Witzler. In 1927 the Gendron Wheel Company was also absorbed by American National. By the 1930s American National was the largest manufacturer of children's vehicles in the world and exported pedal cars into twenty-eight different countries. Other company products included wagons, scooters, hand cars, velocipedes, baby and doll carriages, sleds, playground equipment, invalid chairs, and hospital

Child movie stars were sometimes employed to appear in pedal car advertising as seen in this American National Company ad from 1923 (Courtesy John Rastall)

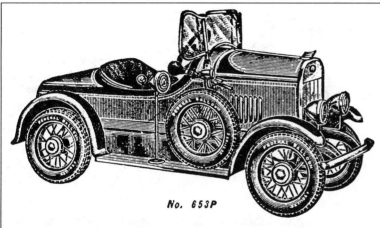

No. 653P

CADILLAC—All Steel Chassis.

Each

‡**No. 653P—SPOKE WHEELS;** Tangent Spokes; Chromium Plated Gigantic Hubs and Caps; 2.50x12.75 Federal Balloon PNEUMATIC Tires (Inflate to 25 lbs. Pressure) SIX WHEELS Furnished as Regular Equipment, the Two Spare Wheels Mounted on Running Boards $90.50

‡**No. 653—DISC WHEELS;** Enameled Sun Tan; 12 in. Special Balloon Type with 1 in. Auto Tread Rubber Tires; Nickel Plated Hub Caps; FIVE WHEELS Furnished as Regular Equipment, One Spare Wheel Mounted on Rear Carrier.................... 68.00

One in a Crate; Weight per Crate 130 lbs.

LENGTH—59 in.

FINISH—Sun Tan, Trimmed with Black, Striped with Coral; Aluminum Molding; Fenders Enameled Sun Tan, with Black Panels.

EQUIPMENT—Chromium Plated Radiator, Upholstered Leather Seat, Instrument Board, Onyx Gear Shift Knob, French Horn, Large Headlights with Emblem, Large Running Board Spot Light, Nickel Plated Tubular Bumpers, (Front and Rear), Oil Can and Bracket; Also Blue-Streak Motor Hummer.

GEAR—Cantilever Springs, Front and Rear; Ball Bearing Rear Axle Brackets; Adjustable Rubber Pedals.

WHEELS—Ball Bearing.

A page from the 1930 American National catalog

A CONDENSED HISTORY
OF AMERICAN PEDAL CAR
MANUFACTURERS

equipment. During peak production, which was prior to Christmas, it was not unusual for the company to have 2800 employees. The factory would operate twenty-four hours a day to fill orders for Santa Claus. American National was the first to introduce streamlining into children's vehicles with the Skippy Airflow Chrysler. The Skippy line also featured Ford, Chevrolet, and Pontiac pedal cars that were faithfully patterned after the actual cars of the day. American National Company's slogan was, "Raise the kiddies on wheels."

Walter Diemer, former president of the company, summed it up best in 1935 when he said, "It's really great fun, this business of ours. It's great fun for us to think that we are making something which gives so much pleasure to so many youngsters." One must remember that during this time the country was experiencing the Great Depression. Unfortunately, by April of 1939 American National had sustained a heavy loss as a result of its operations. The firm was reorganized, bonds were issued, and management control was given to a voting trust. Production continued until the Second World War began. It was the beginning of the war effort and the end of an era for American National.

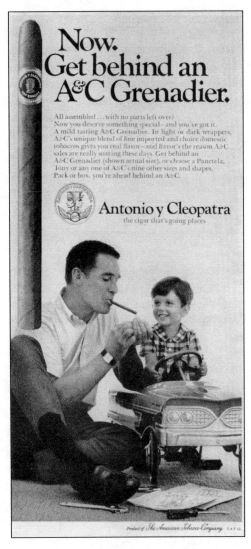

A cigar and a pedal car seem an unlikely combination to be placed in an advertisement together; however, besides manufacturing pedal cars, AMF also produced cigar-making machines. To AMF's chagrin, the ad agency used a T-Bird (Tee Bird) pedal car made by Murray in this particular ad. (Courtesy John Rastall)

AMF

Founded in 1900, American Machine and Foundry built itself up to become the largest producer of cigarette and cigar making and packing machinery in the world. AMF also manufactured baking machinery and automatic pinsetters for bowling alleys. For many years AMF had dabbled in the wheel goods business but decided to aggressively pursue other manufacturing interests. By the early 1950s AMF had nineteen plants and employed more than eleven thousand people. AMF was financially very powerful by 1954 and was able to buy out BMC (a maker of pedal toys) for an undisclosed amount. BMC then became a wholly owned AMF subsidiary. Over the next few years AMF would have to decide which area of its operations had the most potential for new growth.

AMF wasn't the only organization concerned about growth. The year was 1960 and the Olney, Illinois, Chamber of Commerce was wrestling with a problem. The area needed a major industry that would create a sizable amount of jobs; however, new companies weren't exactly rushing into town and posting "help wanted" signs. The solution was to offer 128 acres of land at no cost to the company that could guarantee 500 new jobs. A little over a year later the chosen company was identified as American Machine and Foundry. AMF invested $5,000,000 to build a 490,000 square foot production and warehouse facility. The plant opened in 1962 and began producing tricycles, pedal cars, and pedal tractors. AMF had found its new growth industry and did it ever grow. By 1963, according to *Factory Magazine*, the factory ranked fourteenth in the nation as an outstanding new factory. During 1965 AMF had 700 employees with an annual payroll exceeding $3,000,000. Some of AMF's best known products were the Mustang pedal car and the AMF Firefighter 505 and 508 pedal cars. Several expansions during the late '60s and early '70s increased the plant to a gigantic 715,000 square feet—nearly 16-1/2 acres in size. Production continued for several years and was still going well in 1980 with 900 employees on the payroll. Change was on the horizon, however, and in 1982 AMF sold their operations to Roadmaster Industries, Inc. Roadmaster Industries then acquired Roadmaster Corporation, which had made bicycles for many years. In 1988 the Ajay Enterprises Corporation was purchased by and merged with Roadmaster Corporation. Ajay had made exercise equipment, which Roadmaster wanted to add to its product line. Roadmaster now manufactured fitness equipment such as exercise bikes, treadmills, rowing machines, and weight lifting products along with a full line of bicycles, tricycles, wagons, and plastic riding toys. The company continued to expand and in 1989 bought the Hamilton Lamp Corporation. Hamilton is one of the leading U.S. manufacturers of residential lighting fixtures. In addition, Roadmaster was awarded a contract to make baby strollers for Fisher-Price. Today, Roadmaster employs about 1100 workers at the Olney plant under the direction of Ed Shake. Unlike the other major pedal car manufacturers, Roadmaster still makes pedal cars, even if they are plastic.

The "Mark" in wheel goods

BINGHAMPTON MANUFACTURING CORPORATION

On October 13, 1944, a small tool shop in Binghampton, New York, began producing lock wrenches. In 1947 the shop decided to manufacture something a little more exciting—toy wheel goods. Thus the Binghampton Manufacturing Cor-

BMC first began building wheeled toys in 1947 and had a catalog available for 1948. This ad from the mid-1950s touts the toughness of BMC's products. (Courtesy John Rastall)

A CONDENSED HISTORY
OF AMERICAN PEDAL CAR
MANUFACTURERS

A "Challenger Fire Chief" sold in a 1954 BMC catalog

poration, also known as BMC, was born. During the next several years, BMC became one of the largest producers of children's pedal cars, tractors, bicycles, and tricycles in the United States. Company ads touted that BMC stood for the "Bike & Motor Club." At one time during the early 1950s, BMC had two buildings occupying more than 125,000 square feet of space with a work force of 300.

Surprisingly, in a purely business decision that occurred in March of 1954, Saul W. Botnick, BMC president, announced that the company had been sold to the AMF Corporation. Work continued at the plant for several years until eventually AMF dropped the BMC name and melded BMC's operations to produce AMF products.

GARTON TOY COMPANY

The year was 1879 and two men, E. B. Garton and James Logan, decided to buy some property in Sheboygan, Wiscon-

Garton Toy Company, circa 1891 (Courtesy Toledo Library)

sin, in order to start their own business. The small building they purchased measured only thirty by fifty feet and was formerly the Sheboygan Manufacturing Company. Located along the Sheboygan River and equipped as a planing mill, the men began making cigar boxes, fish boxes, washboards, and other wood items. Business steadily grew and in a few years the partners were able to acquire the rights to manufacture several products no longer being made by the Sheboygan Carriage Company. These products included wheel goods such as wagons and velocipedes.

By 1887 the Garton Toy Company was incorporated with E. B. Garton installed as president. Hard work was beginning

All three Garton Toy Company plants as they appeared in 1938 (Courtesy Toledo Library)

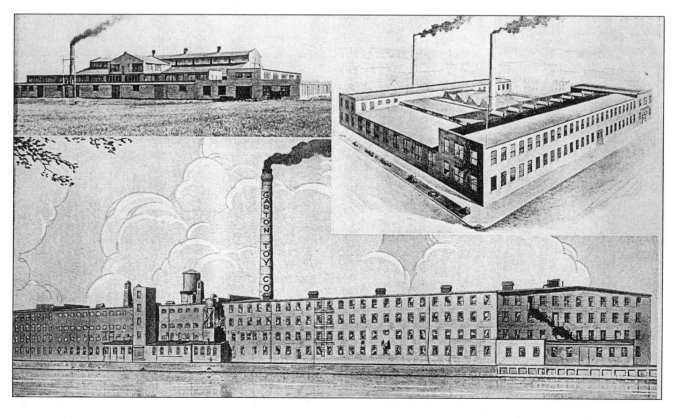

A CONDENSED HISTORY
OF AMERICAN PEDAL CAR
MANUFACTURERS

*The "Dragnet" Auto as featured in the 1957
Garton Toy Company catalog. Notice the electric
microphone and loudspeaker.*

to pay off and business was booming until a disastrous fire struck in 1890. Heartbroken but not defeated, Garton built a new and much larger facility on Niagara Avenue and North Water Street. Over the years this plant produced a wide variety of children's toys such as wagons, velocipedes, scooters, pedal cars, bikes, sleds, and croquet sets.

Then in 1929, disaster struck again when the Garton Toy Company burned to the ground in what was then the largest fire in Sheboygan's history. Then eighty-seven years old and having gone through two major fires in his life, Mr. Garton moved his business into a group of recently vacated buildings. These modern buildings were formerly occupied by the American Hide and Leather Company and in only three months Garton resumed full production. While still president of his toy company, Mr. Garton died in 1931 and left control of the firm to his son, C. E. Garton. The company continued to manufacture pedal cars through the 1930s, including the graceful Lincoln Zephyr model.

During World War II, Garton, like most manufacturing facilities in the U.S., converted to production for the war effort. After the war, toy production resumed and Garton maintained branch offices and showrooms in New York, Chicago, Dallas, San Francisco, and Seattle. By the 1950s the Garton Kidillac and Hot Rod were popular pedal cars and Garton products were being sold in many foreign countries, including Australia and South Africa. Sales were so good, in fact, that in 1961 Garton built a 320,000 square foot facility on seventy-seven acres in the Town of Mosel. Production continued and the company did well until the early 1970s. Then in 1973, due to inadequate profit margins, a declining market, and increased governmental and consumer protection regulations, the Garton Toy Company was sold to the Monitor Corporation. The word "toy" was dropped from the corporate name and by 1975 the Garton Company began assembling lawn and garden tractors out of the former Kingsbury brewery. An additional deal was made to sell the Mosel plant to the Kohler Company to convert for generator production. The Garton Company, after restructuring, did not last and in November of 1976 suspended operations indefinitely. One of the remaining grandsons of E. B. Garton is still alive, though in failing health. It is rumored that he still has a garage full of Garton toys and parts at his home. When the mood strikes him, usually in the summertime, Mr. Garton has a garage sale in which he sells toy items at the price originally marked on the carton. Supposedly, a stranger passing through town a few years ago bought from Mr. Garton several old Garton wagons new in the box. I personally spoke to Mr. Garton, who stated he had nothing to say and wished to maintain his privacy.

GENDRON WHEEL COMPANY

There once was a hard-working French Canadian boy named Pierre Gendron, born on February 23, 1844. At age eleven he labored in a wool-processing mill in Massachusetts and assisted his father, who was a wagonmaker. When Pierre was twenty-one he brought his wife to Toledo and accepted a job as a patternmaker. Pierre worked for six years for Russell & Thayer, which owned the Toledo Novelty Works. Pierre preferred the American equivalent of his name, which was Peter, and that's what his coworkers called him. In 1871 Mr. Gendron moved to Detroit and accepted a job as a patternmaker with the Detroit Safe Company. It was in Detroit that Gendron discovered a method that he was able to patent for making wire wheels. The process involved putting wire spokes in a metal rim and made Gendron a pioneer in the development of the wire wheel. He returned to Toledo in 1877 and tried out his new wheels on baby carriages. At first, Gendron tried to set up a little factory with three other work-

A rare photo of Pierre Gendron. He can be considered the father of the wheel goods industry. (Courtesy Toledo Library)

An 1880 illustration of the Gendron Iron Wheel Company (Courtesy Toledo Library)

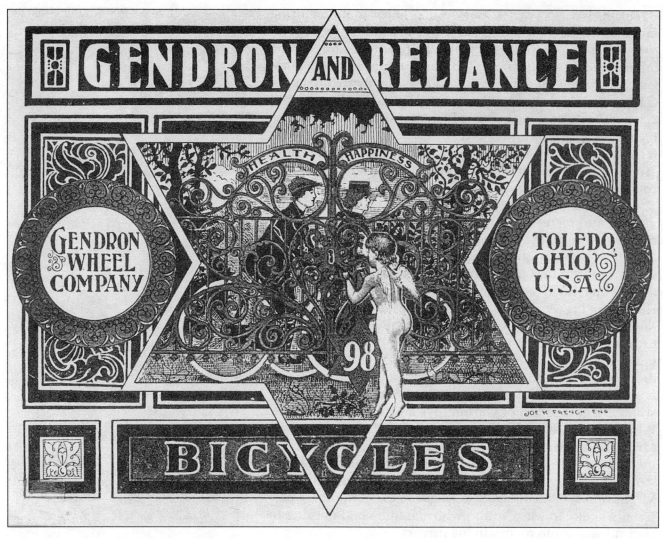

Before Gendron was producing pedal cars, the company made wheels and bicycles (Courtesy Toledo Library)

men in the north end of Toledo. The team attempted to build velocipedes but soon ran out of money. Determined not to give up, Gendron began building baby carriages out of his own home and was able to pay existing debts. Gendron had a lot of faith in his wheels and in 1880 he organized the Gendron Iron Wheel Company at 218 Summit Street, Toledo, Ohio.

By 1882 Gendron invented a lighter and stronger wheel that was less expensive to produce. Due to the success of that wheel, which was primarily used on bicycles, the factory was relocated to Superior and Orange Streets. Sales continued and by the turn of the century the company dropped the word "iron" from its name.

Now the Gendron Wheel Company proudly advertised its Toledo plant as "the world's largest factory devoted to the making of children's vehicles." Gendron products included pedal cars, wagons, scooters, bicycles, baby carriages, doll carriages, and wheelchairs for invalids. Mr. Gendron held twenty-five patents, which included the first iron wagon and steel velocipede. The early 1920s were the heyday for Gendron as products were being shipped to every part of the Unit-

BE SURE YOU ASK
FOR AND GET
THE GENUINE

Full line on display at our
Salesroom, 518 Superior
Street   also for sale in all
of Toledo's best Retail
Stores.

Suggestions
for
Christmas.

*A Christmas ad for Gendron products (Courtesy
Toledo Library)*

ed States and beyond. The company's "Pioneer Line" of children's vehicles became world famous. Advertising of the time stated, "Always ask to see the Gendron Line," and "Be sure you ask for and get the genuine—Gendron." In 1927 Gendron merged with the American National Corporation; however, the Toledo plant continued operation until 1938 when it was abandoned. A reorganization in 1940 changed Gendron's production to that of hospital equipment and located the company in Perrysburg, Ohio. After eighteen years at that location, Gendron moved to Archbold, Ohio, into a modern factory with about sixty employees. In 1964 the Howe Sound Company of New York purchased Gendron.

Today, although a shadow of its former self and no longer in the pedal car business, Gendron still remains in the business of making wheelchairs.

GRAHOUN VEHICLE COMPANY

Produced wheel goods in the early 1900s, including the "Rundal" pedal car. The factory was located in Fremont, Ohio.

HAMILTON STEEL PRODUCTS

Located at 1845 West 74th Street in Chicago, Illinois, Hamilton produced wagons, scooters, garden carts, hand tools, and children's automobiles. It is believed the company was started in the early 1950s, and by 1966 Hamilton employed 110 men and 100 women in its Chicago factory. The company president at that time was S. Ward Hamilton, Jr. Pedal car enthusiasts remember one of the company's most famous products—the Hamilton pedal jeep.

*A diagram showing the features of the Irish Mail
(Courtesy Elkhart Library)*

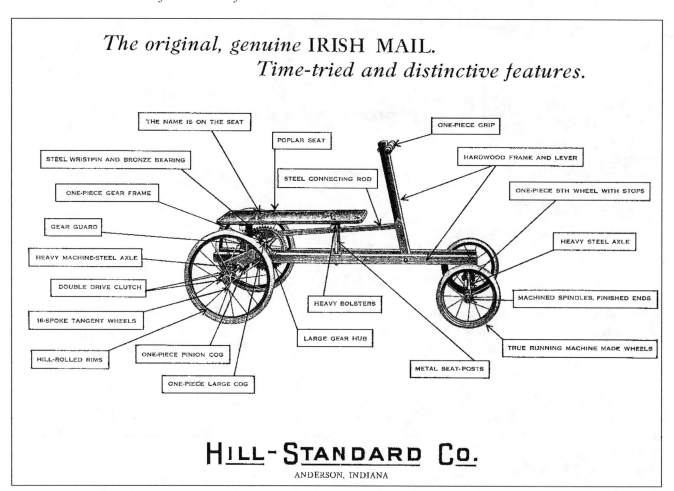

The original, genuine IRISH MAIL.
Time-tried and distinctive features.

THE NAME IS ON THE SEAT

ONE-PIECE GRIP

STEEL WRISTPIN AND BRONZE BEARING

POPLAR SEAT

HARDWOOD FRAME AND LEVER

ONE-PIECE GEAR FRAME

STEEL CONNECTING ROD

ONE-PIECE 5TH WHEEL WITH STOPS

GEAR GUARD

HEAVY STEEL AXLE

HEAVY MACHINE-STEEL AXLE

DOUBLE DRIVE CLUTCH

HEAVY BOLSTERS

MACHINED SPINDLES, FINISHED ENDS

16-SPOKE TANGENT WHEELS

LARGE GEAR HUB

TRUE RUNNING MACHINE MADE WHEELS

HILL-ROLLED RIMS

ONE-PIECE PINION COG

METAL SEAT-POSTS

ONE-PIECE LARGE COG

HILL-STANDARD CO.
ANDERSON, INDIANA

HILL-STANDARD MANUFACTURING COMPANY

The year was 1900 and inventor Hugh Hill had been working on a prototype for a children's riding toy that had four wheels and was propelled by moving a lever back and forth with the rider's arms. Mr. Hill called his new invention the "Irish Mail." Thus the Hill Tool Company was formed, which later became Hill-Standard Manufacturing Company. Located in Anderson, Indiana, Hill-Standard became one of the world's largest manufacturer of lightweight metal wheels. The company also made velocipedes, tricycles, and sulkies, but it didn't take long for the Irish Mail to become the company's best-selling item and to gain worldwide popularity. By 1914, Hill-Standard was turning out fifteen thousand wire wheels per day and a large quantity of children's vehicles, including pedal cars. Besides the Irish Mail, two other well-known models of hand cars that Hill-Standard made were the "Green Dragon" and the "Ben Hur Racer." Soon the company was able to add playground equipment such as slides, see-saws, and a junior gymnasium to its product line. An additional factory was opened in Kokomo, Indiana, to maintain production levels. The company continued with great success through the 1920s until it went out of business during the Depression.

KIRK LATTY MANUFACTURING

Located at 1971 West 85th Street in Cleveland, Ohio, Kirk Latty was a manufacturer of fasteners in the late 1890s and early 1900s. By the First World War the company offered a complete line of wheel goods, including tricycles, hand cars, and pedal cars. The company enjoyed success for many years and in 1926 merged with Lamson and Sessions. Lamson and Sessions was one of the nation's leading fastener manufacturers and started out in 1866 making carriage bolts. It is believed that wheel goods production was discontinued when the two companies merged.

MASON & PARKER

Turn-of-the-century manufacturer of wheel goods, which operated out of Winchendon, Massachusetts. The company offered a small line of pedal cars and was still in business as late as 1907.

MIDWEST INDUSTRIES

In 1932, Theo Moll, Emil Jochum, and Erwin Gerhard founded Modern Tool & Die in Cleveland, Ohio. The thrust of the company's operations catered to the bicycle and automotive industry. For many years the company performed well and by the 1950s was ready to expand its product line.

A CONDENSED HISTORY
OF AMERICAN PEDAL CAR
MANUFACTURERS

*A 1957 Jet Hawk Sportster by Midwest (Courtesy
John Rastall)*

In 1953 a new division of MTD was created, known as Midwest Industries. Midwest was located in Willard, Ohio, and produced children's wheel goods, such as tricycles and wagons. Bicycles were later added to the product line.

By 1956 the company began producing pedal cars; however, only three versions of pedal cars were offered from a single stamping. These were a sportster, a hook and ladder, and a fire chief's car. Midwest's flagship pedal car was a sportster known as the "Jet Hawk." Loosely styled after the Studebaker Hawk, the Jet Hawk featured fins, a large chrome hood ornament, and a "jewel lustered flamboyant" paint scheme. Pedal car production continued until 1962. Other wheel goods that Midwest manufactured were discontinued after 1972.

Today, Modern Tool & Die is still in business. In fact, MTD is the largest supplier of outdoor power equipment in the world. Most major hardware stores and home centers carry lawnmowers, garden tillers, snowblowers, and other equipment that are produced by MTD. Modern Tool & Die is a true success story, founded in the Depression, involved in growth industries over the years, and headed on a steady course for the twenty-first century.

MONARCH PRODUCTS COMPANY

The Monarch Products Company was a small manufacturer of washboards and after having limited success making this type of woodenware, Monarch began producing children's vehicles. Judging from a few pieces of rare catalog literature, Monarch offered what appeared to be several deluxe models of pedal cars. Information on the company is sketchy mainly because it was in business for only a short time. It is known that the company was based in Tiffin, Ohio, and had ties to the Toledo area. Monarch Products was listed in old city directories between 1930 and 1934. By 1936 the plant was shut down and the property was sold. Company officers included F. B. Cramer, president; J. C. Meyers, vice president; and J. P. Schmitz, secretary-treasurer.

MURRAY OHIO MANUFACTURING COMPANY

In the early 1900s a number of fledgling companies were producing or at least attempting to produce automobiles. This new automotive industry was centered in Detroit, Michigan, with a majority of suppliers located in the surrounding area. One of the suppliers that provided parts to the automotive industry was the Murray Body Company.

Founded in 1910 by J. W. Murray, the company operated out of Detroit. Business was going well and in 1919 the company needed to expand by building another plant. A suitable site was found in Cleveland, Ohio, and stocks were sold to help finance the project. The new plant was called Murray Ohio and was under the control of C. W. Hannon. Mr. Hannon was the son-in-law of J. W. Murray. Items that were made at the new plant included fenders, gas tanks, and various sheet metal parts for the Chandler Motor Car Company; however, it wasn't long before Chandler Motors was in financial trouble, which meant the new Murray plant was also feeling the economic crunch. Fortunately, Murray Body Company was doing a brisk parts business with Chevrolet and was able to assign part of the work to the Murray Ohio factory. Mr. Murray was concerned about his business and did not want to rely solely on the automotive industry.

It was apparent that Murray had to protect itself economically by branching out into other product lines. Fortunately, a new product line presented itself when the White Truck Company wanted a miniature model of their product. Murray created a small replica and White Truck liked the results, which gave Murray the confidence it needed and in 1923 the company decided to enter the children's wheel goods business. By 1924 Murray Ohio had produced two different pedal cars and one steel coaster wagon. Since more space was required, Murray Ohio purchased a factory on 152nd Street in Cleveland. This new plant began making pedal cars, or juvenile automobiles as they were commonly called, under the name "Steelcraft." Meanwhile, the Murray Body Company merged with three other companies and began experiencing financial trouble.

To gain much needed cash, the Murray Body Company agreed to sell its controlling interest in Murray Ohio for $200,000. When Murray Ohio became independent in 1925, it continued to manufacture sheet metal parts for several automotive companies. Murray also continued to make children's pedal cars and in 1927 began making velocipedes.

THE FAMOUS  AUTOS AND TRACTORS

Model M-740 — Fire Truck
Full Ball Bearing

DIMENSIONS: Length 47", width 17"
WHEELS: Ball bearing, 8" double disc. Yellow with black trim
DRIVING MECHANISM: Ball bearing pull straps, ball bearing rear axle
  hangers
FIRE CHIEF BELL: Bright plated
HAND RAIL: Two tubular rails, baked yellow enamel
WINDSHIELD: Yellow
TIRES: 1" solid rubber   PEDALS: Rubber block
LADDERS: Two wooden varnished ladders
SEAT PAD: Fabric type, yellow
FINISH: Body in vermilion and white baked enamel. Side panels white
  with fathom blue trim. Bumper aluminum enamel
PACKING: One per carton. Shipping weight 37 lbs.

Model M-741 — Ranch Wagon
Full Ball Bearing

DIMENSIONS: Length 47", width 17"
WHEELS: Ball bearing, 8" double disc, vermilion with white trim
DRIVING MECHANISM: Ball bearing pull straps, ball bearing rear axle
  hangers
BUMPER: Front bumper aluminum baked enamel
RADIATOR ORNAMENT: Bright plated
WINDSHIELD: Aluminum enameled
HANDRAILS: Tubular steel enameled aluminum
SEAT PAD: Fabric type in vermilion
TIRES: 1" solid rubber   PEDALS: Rubber block
FINISH: Body in mecca blue with peacock blue baked enamel body panels
PACKING: One per carton. Shipping weight 37 lbs.

Model M-742 — Dump Truck
Full Ball Bearing

DIMENSIONS: Length 47", width 17"
WHEELS: Ball bearing, 8" double disc, yellow with black trim
DRIVING MECHANISM: Ball bearing pull straps, ball bearing rear axle
  hangers
BUMPER: Front bumper aluminum baked enamel
RADIATOR ORNAMENT: Bright plated
WINDSHIELD: Black baked enamel
DUMP BOX: Easily operated from seat position
SEAT PAD: Fabric type in black
TIRES: 1" solid rubber   PEDALS: Rubber block
FINISH: Body in yellow baked enamel. Side panels black enamel
  with white trim
PACKING: One per carton. Shipping weight 38 lbs.

Model M-621 — Fire Truck
Full Ball Bearing

BODY: New 1956 body styling
DIMENSIONS: Length 43", width 17"
WHEELS: Ball bearing, 8" double disc, vermilion with white trim
DRIVING MECHANISM: Ball bearing pull straps, ball bearing rear axle
  hangers
FIRE CHIEF BELL: Bright plated
HAND RAILS: Steel white baked enamel
LADDERS: Two wooden varnished ladders
TIRES: 5/8" solid rubber
SEAT PAD: Fabric type, yellow
FINISH: Body in vermilion baked enamel, side panels in white,
  fathom blue trim. Aluminum grille
PACKING: One per carton, Shipping weight 34 lbs.

Two pages of pedal cars and velocipedes sold in the 1956 Murray Wheel Goods Catalogue

THE FAMOUS  VELOCIPEDES

Model M-400
Front Wheel Ball Bearing

FRAME: 1¼" tubular, heavy gauge steel, hydrogen brazed.
PEDAL: Block rubber.
HANDLEBAR: ¾" adjustable, white baked enamel.
SADDLE: Metal adjustable.
WHEELS: Heavy gauge machine spoke, front wheel ball bearing.
GRIPS: Red plastic.
TIRES: 1½" semi-pneumatic front and rear.
FINISH: Frame, saddle, fork, platform in vermilion baked enamel with white trim. Wheels, fender and handlebar in white baked enamel.
PACKING: One per carton.

SIZES	FRONT WHEEL	REAR WHEELS	WEIGHT
MODEL M-400	10"	7"	17 lbs.
MODEL M-401	12"	8"	19 lbs.
MODEL M-402	16"	10"	23 lbs.

Model M-385
Front Wheel Ball Bearing

FRAME: 1¼" tubular, heavy gauge steel, hydrogen brazed.
PEDALS: Block rubber.
HANDLEBAR: ¾" adjustable, white baked enamel.
SADDLE: Metal adjustable.
WHEELS: Heavy gauge machine spoke, front wheel ball bearing.
GRIPS: Red plastic.
TIRES: ¾" solid rubber.
FINISH: Frame, fork, fender, platform in vermilion baked enamel. Wheels and saddle in white baked enamel. White trim.
PACKING: One per carton.

SIZES	FRONT WHEEL	REAR WHEELS	WEIGHT
MODEL M-385	10"	6"	14 lbs.
MODEL M-386	12"	8"	15 lbs.
MODEL M-387	16"	10"	16 lbs.

Model M-380
Front Wheel Ball Bearing

FRAME: 1¼" tubular, heavy gauge steel, hydrogen brazed.
PEDALS: Block rubber.
HANDLEBAR: ¾" adjustable white baked enamel.
SADDLE: Metal adjustable.
WHEELS: Heavy gauge machine spoke, front wheel ball bearing.
GRIPS: Red plastic.
TIRES: ⅝" solid rubber.
FINISH: Frame, fork, platform, saddle in vermilion baked enamel. Wheels white baked enamel.
PACKING: One per carton.

SIZES	FRONT WHEEL	REAR WHEELS	WEIGHT
MODEL M-380	10"	6"	13 lbs.

Model M-111 — Murray-Go-Round
Full Ball Bearing

FRAME: Tubular steel
SEAT: Acid resistant enamel
TIRES: Semi-pneumatic rubber
BUMPERS: Flexible steel, white rubber covered
PLAY BEADS: Wood, non-toxic color finish
BRAKE: Sure action, easily operated
PUSH HANDLE: Adjustable, chrome plated
PACKAGE CARRIER: Large capacity, steel wire
FINISH: Peacock blue baked enamel
PACKING: One per carton
SHIPPING WEIGHT: 25 lbs.

FORKS: Non-shimmy
WHEELS: Ball bearing

As with many other companies of the day, the Great Depression had a devastating effect on Murray Ohio. In fact, if it wasn't for pedal cars and other wheeled toy sales, the company would have gone out of business. The 1930s were tough, but Murray was able to build a strong sales force and had accounts all across the nation.

In 1936 Murray decided to add yet another line of wheeled items under the name of "Mercury." The Mercury line would mainly feature bicycles and wagons. By 1940, Murray had completely stopped producing automotive parts and concentrated on pedal cars, wagons, bicycles, velocipedes, and window fans.

When World War II began, the government ordered that production of civilian products be cut back drastically. To help the war effort and to preserve itself as a company, Murray Ohio began making magazines for anti-aircraft guns and 100-pound bombs. After the war there was a large demand for pedal cars, bicycles, and fans. For the 1950 model year the Murray line of wheeled toys was completely restyled and ball-bearing wheels were used extensively.

Trouble was on the horizon, though, as imported English bicycles were driving the price of Murray bikes down. In the meantime, Murray was still paying union worker's wages, which were not in step with the current market. As Murray saw it, they could either go out of business or move the company to an area where "economic conditions were more favorable." A decision was made to move the company to Lawrenceburg, Tennessee, and the project was completed by April of 1956.

The plant produced many products and underwent several expansions over the years. By 1960 the factory and offices took up 828,600 square feet. Murray began producing lightweight bicycles and new children's vehicles such as the tot rod. In 1967 the company began producing lawnmowers and found them to be in growing demand. Reluctantly, in 1973 Murray Ohio decided to get out of the pedal car business. This decision was based on economics. Bicycles and lawnmowers were selling extremely well and had great growth potential; on the other hand, pedal cars had only a small profit margin and showed little growth potential. Murray continued to produce bicycles and lawnmowers and is still in business today. Now called Murray International, the company is the number one producer of affordable lawnmowers in the U.S.

SIDWAY-TOPLIFF COMPANY

In the 1890s in Chicago, a man named Harry Sidway began making baby buggies, strollers, velocipedes, and scooters; however, the real story begins with a relative of Harry Sidway. That man was Charles A. Sidway. Born in Jackson, Mississippi, on October 11, 1878, Charles soon moved to Nashville, Tennessee,

Cover of the 1929 Sidway-Topliff Company toy catalog

and when he was eighteen years old he traveled to Chicago and started working for his cousin, Harry Sidway. By 1904, when Charles Sidway was twenty-seven years old, he wanted to try his hand at running his own small manufacturing company. With $500.00 he borrowed, Charles Sidway was able to rent a 40 foot by 80 foot building that was formerly used to make bedside tables. The company was successful and soon other items were added to the product line, including card tables, shaving and toilet stands, costumers, umbrella racks, and baby carriages. Growth was phenomenal and by 1910 the Sidway Mercantile Company was the largest company in Elkhart. The plant covered seven acres and employed 550 workers.

One day while Charles Sidway was checking the plant he noticed a man named Timmerhoff tinkering at his workbench during his lunch break. It appeared Timmerhoff was making a fold-up cart for his daughter. Immediately Sidway was interested and asked Timmerhoff to show him how it worked. After seeing the demonstration, Mr. Sidway recognized that the go-cart design was ingenious and told Timmerhoff to forget his other work and devote all of his time to this new invention. In no time, the plant began manufacturing the new go-cart. Mr. Sidway helped Timmerhoff secure a patent on this item and paid him a royalty on each go-cart produced. These go-carts were made under the trade name of "Alwin." A unique feature of the manufacturing process was its use of spot welds, for which Sidway had obtained the exclusive rights. By 1915 Charles Sidway was a very rich man and a young one at that. He seemed to have it all, a successful business, a wonderful family, and lots of friends—but something wasn't quite right. Ever since he had his appendix removed several years earlier, Mr. Sidway was plagued with bothersome intestinal lesions. He was advised by his physicians to go to New York for an operation. The day following the operation Mr. Sidway contracted pneumonia and died. He left behind a wife and three children. When the factory got word of his death, the plant closed for two days out of respect for their former boss. Folks remembered how the kind-hearted Mr. Sidway supplied coal for needy Elkhart families to keep warm in the winter.

Manufacturing continued and headquarters were moved to Washington, Pennsylvania, in 1926. Sidway-Topliff now had two other factories, one in Elkhart, Indiana, and the other in Toronto, Ontario. The company specialized in children's vehicles, velocipedes, and doll carriages, and began to pick up momentum in the late 1920s. Unfortunately, when the stock market crashed in 1929, so did the Sidway-Topliff company. According to Bob Moore, a local toy collector from Washington, Pennsylvania, information on Sidway is scarce. Bob fondly remembers playing behind the Sidway factory when he was a boy. It seemed almost every day workers would discard damaged wheels and unusable wicker from the manufacturing process. A large pile would be made and later burned. Bob and his friends would sneak behind the plant and gather up wheels and other odds and ends to try to assemble their own playthings. By 1930 activity ceased and the company closed its doors forever. Today the old factory still stands, with the current tenants selling plumbing supplies.

Steelcraft's Supercharger and Pursuit Plane from 1941

STEELCRAFT

In 1924, Murray Ohio purchased a factory on 152nd Street in Cleveland. The factory would be used to manufacture pedal cars and other wheel goods under the trade name of "Steelcraft." Other products included steel coaster wagons and three-wheeled velocipedes. The Steelcraft line was a good seller and helped sustain Murray Ohio through the Depression. Steelcraft offered many varieties of pedal cars that are popular with collectors and restorers. These models include the Streamliner and Super Charger, the Chrysler Airflow, the Lincoln Zephyr, Pontiac and Chrysler automobiles, and the Pursuit Plane. Sears, Roebuck and Company used the name "Boycraft" to sell their own line of wheel goods made by Steelcraft. By the mid-1950s, the Steelcraft name was no longer marketed. See also Murray Ohio.

TOLEDO METAL WHEEL COMPANY

Founded in 1887 in the Toledo area by Frank Southard, the Toledo Metal Wheel Company was one of several companies that manufactured bicycle and velocipede wheels. By 1901, the company had a line of pedal cars, including the "Toledo" automobile. The company billed itself as the largest producer of wire wheel goods in the world with the motto, "The survival of the fittest." As time went on, Toledo continued to

A department store display from 1938 shows a nice selection of Steelcraft pedal cars. In this time period, wheel goods topped sales of all other toys at Christmas. (Courtesy John Rastall)

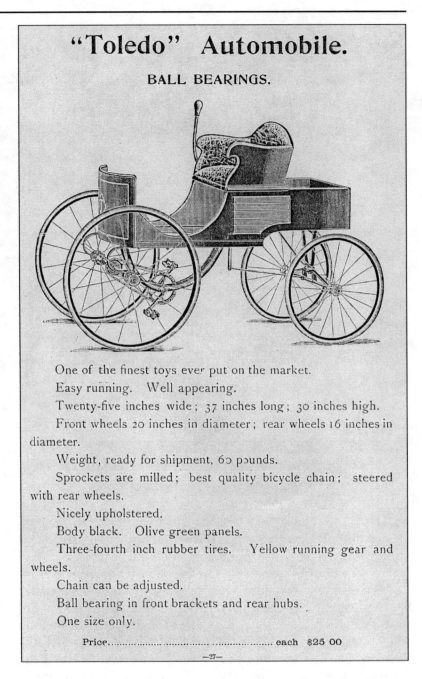

"Toledo" Automobile.

BALL BEARINGS.

One of the finest toys ever put on the market.

Easy running.   Well appearing.

Twenty-five inches wide; 37 inches long; 30 inches high.

Front wheels 20 inches in diameter; rear wheels 16 inches in diameter.

Weight, ready for shipment, 60 pounds.

Sprockets are milled; best quality bicycle chain; steered with rear wheels.

Nicely upholstered.

Body black.   Olive green panels.

Three-fourth inch rubber tires.   Yellow running gear and wheels.

Chain can be adjusted.

Ball bearing in front brackets and rear hubs.

One size only.

Price.. each $25 00

—27—

A 1901 pedal car manufactured by the Toledo Metal Wheel Company. Note the tiller steering. (Courtesy John Rastall)

manufacture pedal cars with the slogan, "The car that grows with your child." At least two lines of pedal cars were available, the "Blue Streak line", and the "Super Quality line." Further details of the company's history is sketchy; however, it is known that the company was purchased by American National in the mid-1920s. See also The American National Company.

Section II

How to Restore Your

PEDAL CAR

A Step-By-Step Procedures Guide

PEDAL CAR RESTORATION PROCESS

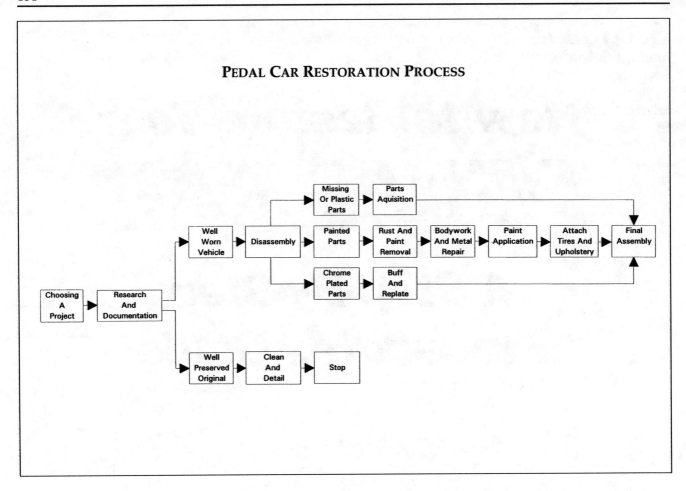

A LOGICAL APPROACH TO RESTORATION

For anyone working on a restoration project, things go along much more smoothly by following a plan and taking it step-by-step. In most cases it is better to accomplish certain restoration steps before further steps are taken. This is not to say that there is only one correct way to restore a pedal car; however, there is a logical approach whereby each step sensibly follows the one before it. It is possible to separate the restoration process of a pedal car into nine steps:

1. Choosing a project
2. Research and documentation
3. Disassembly and paint matching
4. Rust and paint removal
5. Parts acquisition and plating
6. Bodywork and metal repair
7. Paint application
8. Tires and upholstery
9. Final assembly

Each of these steps will involve a series of smaller steps to achieve the desired goals. Some steps, such as parts acquisition, are "floating" and can be started at the option of the restorer after completing a few initial stages.

The flow chart on the previous page shows the progression of events during a typical pedal car restoration.

SUGGESTED TOOLS AND MATERIALS REQUIRED FOR A PEDAL CAR RESTORATION

Documentation:
- Camera with film
- Notebook and pencil
- Tracing paper

Disassembly:
- Can of rust dissolver such as WD40
- 9/16-inch open end wrench
- Adjustable wrench
- Slotted screwdriver
- Regular pliers
- Needlenose pliers
- Side cutters
- Acrylic hammer
- Ruler
- Power drill
- Drill bits
- Rotary tool with cut-off wheel
- Resealable plastic bags

Rust and Paint Removal:
- Protective clothing
- Goggles
- Respirator
- Rubber gloves
- Aircraft paint stripper
- Brush
- Metal container
- Scraper
- Heat gun
- Coarse steel wool
- Sandblaster
- Silica sand
- Sandpaper
- Wire wheel

Bodywork:	Body hammer
	Dolly
	Ball peen hammer
	Putty knife
	Sanding blocks
	Sandpaper
	Spot putty
	Seam caulk
	Hand drill
	TIG welder
	Welder's mask and gloves
	Welding rod
	Grinder
Paint Supplies:	Drop cloths
	Coveralls
	Respirator
	Mixing sticks
	Containers
	Wire or nylon string
	Paper filter funnels
	Primer/filler
	Lacquer thinner
	Paint (Acrylic enamel)
	Reducer
	Fisheye preventative
	Hardener
	Painter's masking tape
	Spray gun with filter
	Air compressor
	Air hose
	Painter's masking tape
	Exacto knife
	Liquid mask solution
	Newspaper
Tires:	Tire rubber
	Bondini cement
	PVC cutter

Upholstery: Vinyl or leather material
                 Heavy duty thread
                 Commercial sewing machine

Final assembly: Painter's masking tape
                 Slotted screwdriver
                 Adjustable wrench
                 Needlenose pliers
                 Lithium grease
                 Towels
                 Ruler

A NOTE REGARDING SAFETY:

Be sure to read and follow the manufacturer's recommendations when using any type of tool or restoration product. Always wear the proper protective clothing and keep a clean workshop to help prevent injuries.

1940 Gendron Pioneer Roadster patterned after a 1940 Nash. Designed by Brooks Stevens. Owned and restored by Vincent F. Ruffolo.

CHAPTER 4

CHOOSING A PROJECT

One of the first challenges to beset both the novice and advanced enthusiast is choosing a pedal vehicle to restore. Before making a final decision, a wise purchaser will consider several factors, including price, condition, and his or her skill level.

The first thing you need to do is calculate the money that is available for the project. A first time restorer may want to keep the investment low, considering there is always the option of later selling or trading the first pedal car and upgrading to a more expensive and desirable one. Naturally, the price of the pedal car being considered should be carefully evaluated to see if it is comparable to what others have paid for a similar model. Don't hesitate to discuss it with a fellow collector—another person's opinion and perspective may be a valuable resource for you. It would also be prudent to track the prices of various models of pedal cars at shows, auctions, and through classified ads. When negotiating a purchase, let the seller set the asking price and don't be afraid to make a low initial offer. Most sellers "pad" the price because they know the buyer will want to pay a lower purchase price. This is the typical wheeling and dealing that occurs when buying or selling virtually any type of collectible. Expect to pay somewhere between the seller's asking price and your initial offer.

All important to the success of the project is the initial condition of the pedal car. Some pedal cars offered for sale have inflated prices and have been doctored up to look presentable, just like some real cars found at the proverbial "used car lot." Beware of such pitfalls as mismatched wheels, excessive body fillers, patch panels, body marriages, and misrepresented reproductions. Keep in mind that a project that is heavily rusted or pitted will have a greater level of difficulty and will require more time to restore correctly. A common cover-up to hide body damage or heavy pitting is to upholster the inner sides of the pedal car, but whereas this may save time, the resulting effect is a poorer quality restoration. A pedal car in poor condition or with a large number of missing parts will require additional funds, but may turn out to be an excellent candidate for restoration if it is highly sought after because of its rarity.

As a prospective restorer, you also need to assess your skill level. If you have a basic knowledge of hand tools and a moderate amount of patience, much of the restoration can be completed by you. Some restorers prefer to hire out certain parts of the project, like paintwork or welding. This is perfectly acceptable and in some cases necessary. Chromium plating, for example, is not practical to do at home and is best left to a professional plating shop. Obviously, it is more expensive to hire others to complete various phases of your project, so don't be afraid to try your hand at a new skill or procedure. You may surprise yourself and realize that it wasn't so difficult after all.

The project you choose is based on what appeals to you and what your budget will allow. A big-fendered car from the 1920s with a fancy radiator ornament might be what you're able to collect or restore. Maybe the streamlined look of cars from the late 1930s would be appealing to you. How about a car from the 1950s with lots of chrome? On the other hand, as a first project you might decide to restore a car from the 1960s.

If you're buying a pedal car strictly to resell, choose one with the original paint. You probably won't want to completely restore it. Instead, replace any missing or severely damaged parts and thoroughly detail the car. This will allow you the greatest profit margin with the least amount of hours devoted to the project.

Whatever style of pedal car you choose, the key is to have fun during the restoration and to be proud of the completed project. Your finished pedal car will not only give you a good feeling, it will put a smile on the face of those who see it.

After purchasing a pedal car, it is important to determine the level of restoration it needs. If a collector is fortunate enough to find a pedal car in excellent original condition, all that may be needed in the way of restoration is thorough cleaning and detailing of the car. This may require partial disassembly and the use of polishing compounds on the paint. Some pedal cars are found with a satisfactory original finish but are missing trim or other components. In this case it would be better to replace the missing parts and not proceed with refinishing the body.

Some pedal cars have just enough of the original finish to make the decision to repaint them more debatable. As a general rule, if a pedal car retains 60 percent or more of well-preserved original paint it is better to refrain from repainting the body. This does not mean that all pedal cars with a majority of their original paint should not be restored; that is a judgment call and depends on personal preference. In some cases the pedal car will be so weathered and worn that the choice to do a full restoration is an obvious one.

GENERAL GUIDELINES FOR CHOOSING AND BUYING PEDAL CARS:

- Let the buyer beware. Since old pedal cars don't come with a warranty, the buyer takes the risk of authenticity and restorability upon himself.

- Buy the best condition of pedal car that you can find. A pedal car in good, restorable condition will, in the long run, be easier and less expensive to restore.

- It is better to locate a pedal car that is complete. If it has any missing or damaged parts, try to determine before purchasing the car if parts are available.

- Buy the make and model of pedal car that appeals to you the most. Since the style of pedal car that you like is a matter of personal preference, get the car that you really want.

- A pedal car in excellent original condition is preferred over a restored model. This statement is reinforced time and time again at pedal car shows and auctions, where the highest prices realized are usually for unrestored examples in excellent original condition.

- The demand, condition, age, and availability are the prime factors that determine the value of a pedal car.

- Demand for a pedal car is the most important element of price.

- Heavily optioned pedal cars with fine workmanship from the 1920s and 1930s and rare models from short-lived manufacturers are highly sought after.

- A pedal car that mirrors the style of a full-size automobile has an enhanced value to collectors.

- Besides those in the hobby, pedal cars are sought after by antique dealers, toy collectors, auctioneers, bike collectors, and classic car buffs.

- Several styles of pedal cars are currently being reproduced. If there is ever any doubt as to the authenticity of a pedal car, consult a reputable pedal car collector for an expert opinion.

- To restore or not to restore, that is the question.

In order to show the complete restoration of a pedal car in this book, much thought was given to choosing the proper model for a step-by-step guide. First, it was determined that the pedal car should be affordable to the average restorer; therefore, a post-WWII pedal car was deemed to be a good choice, as prewar pedal cars are generally in a higher price bracket. Next, the collectibility had to be considered. The project pedal car should be widely popular to enthusiasts, yet not considered too common. It should also be mainly original so as to show the original paint and keep the expenses for parts at a minimum.

The chosen pedal car was a "Champion" made by Murray Ohio. Sometimes referred to as a "dipside" version, this body style had more side contour than later models and is less common than a straightside Champion. Popular during the 1950s, the Murray Champion is well-remembered by the over forty crowd and is very popular with restorers. The problem now was to find an original dipside Champion that would be a suitable candidate for restoration.

A person can go to scores of garage sales and flea markets in an attempt to find a pedal car for a bargain price. After many frustrating stops, a collector might stumble on a late model pedal car for under $50. In the long run, however, it is less expensive and much easier to attend a pedal car show and make a selection there. Even though the price you pay for a pedal car may be higher than if you found one at a garage sale, the time and aggravation you save will be worth it. When searching for our restoration project, it just so happened that a large pedal car show was due in the area in a few weeks. Since good restorable pedal cars are usually sold quickly, I attended the show as an early bird for an extra admission fee.

Only a handful of Champions were for sale at the show. Some were very overpriced and only two were dipside versions. After deciding which Champion to pursue, I made an offer to the seller and money exchanged hands.

As with most project cars there were some positives and negatives about the Champion that was chosen. On the positive side, it had most of its original paint and graphics. The body and windshield were fairly straight and the underside did not reveal any heavy rust or pitting. All of the trim and undercarriage was in place. A minor accessory, the seat pad, was missing; however, this is typical of most unrestored pedal cars. An added bonus about this project car is that many of the parts for the Champion are being reproduced or are available in used condition. Even the graphics are commercially available.

On the negative side, the body did have quite a number of small dents and several nonoriginal holes that would require extra work to fix properly. It seems the former owner had placed screws in the holes and painted them blue in an attempt to disguise the damage. The back panel of the pedal car had twelve holes of various sizes that made the rear bumper look like Swiss cheese when the screws were removed.

Many of the original fasteners were rusty or had been damaged from improper contact with hand tools. Why is it that when folks worked on a pedal car they never had the proper tool handy and would end up stripping the screw head or nut? As is normal for a restoration project, the plating on the hubcaps and hood ornament was no longer shiny and the tires and pedals were heavily worn and would need to be replaced. This project Champion was medium blue with white trim and was represented as a 1952 model. On the body of the car the original graphics "Champion" and "Jet Flow Drive" could be seen and a Murray Ohio decal was on the back of the seat and was fairly well preserved. The pedal car was transported to the home workshop where the restoration process could begin.

Photograph the pedal car before any work begins. Do this outside, as natural light yields very good results.

CHAPTER 5

RESEARCH AND DOCUMENTATION

Whether you're an advanced collector of pedal cars or have purchased your first project, you need to do your homework. This includes searching out all available information on your particular pedal car. A mere trip to the local library will probably not yield much information and may be disappointing. In the past there have been a few books written on pedal cars, but some of these books are out of print or were focused on European pedal cars. Fortunately, you are now reading this publication.

It is very helpful to locate a copy of an original manufacturer's catalog page featuring your car. Manufacturers' catalogs contained all the specifications for their models of pedal cars, including the available colors and trim. An illustration was provided, usually in color, to show exactly how the car looked when it was brand new. The type of wheels,

An original 1951-52 Murray Ohio wheel goods catalog shows the "Champion" model in full color. Documentation such as this is desirable to obtain before starting the restoration process. It is interesting to note that the company artist's rendering showed the painted area of the grille to be higher than on the original pedal car.

Big, New Values in CHAIN-DRIVE Autos

- More Speed—Easier Riding. Heavy gauge strong steel bodies
- Easy-to-operate chain drive develops more power with less effort
- Ball-bearing rear axle and pedal crank give smoother riding comfort

[A] Fire Chief's Car. Clang, clang—here comes the chief! Enclosed chain drive and features above. Quick turning. Ball-bearing 8-in. double-disc steel wheels. ⅝-in. solid rubber tires. Bright plated bell. Rubber block pedals. Seat pad. Red baked-on enamel finish, yellow and silver color trim. 36x17 in. wide.
79 N 08954L—Shpg. wt. 30 lbs. . . $16.95

[B] Hot-Rod Racer for pint-size speeders! A colorful "souped-up" model. Enclosed chain drive and features listed above. Nylon-bearing 10-inch steel artillery wheels. 1¾-in. semi-pneumatic rubber tires. 2-pc. rubber pedals. Orange baked-on enamel finish, black and white trim. 35 in. long.
79 N 08950L—Shpg. wt. 36 lbs. . . $17.95

[C] Big Dump Truck. Box operates from driver's seat. Tail gate raises, lowers. Lock device holds box. Enclosed chain drive, features above. Ball-bearing 8-in. double-disc steel wheels. ⅝-in. solid rubber tires. Rubber block pedals. Seat pad. Yellow baked-on enamel finish, with dark trim. Plated ornament. Freight, express or truck.
79 N M8965—47x17 in. wide. Shpg. wt. 38 lbs. $21.75

[D] Two-tone "Kidillac" with dash-controlled electric horn and lights. (Battery not included, order below.) Removable spare wheel, rear view mirror. Enclosed chain drive and construction as above. Ball-bearing 8-inch double-disc steel wheels. 1¼-inch rubber tires. 2-piece rubber pedals. Baked-on enamel finish, aluminum trim. 45x20 inches wide.
79 N M8980—Deluxe Model. Electric Head, tail lights, horn. Cream and Blue. Shpg. wt. 52 lbs. $36.95
79 N M8953—Standard Model. (Not shown.) No lights, horn. Chartreuse and red. Wt. 51 lbs. $28.45
34 N 4702—Power-Pak Battery. Shpg. wt. 1 lb. 6 oz. 75c

IMPORTANT
All wheel toys shipped partly assembled to save you money.

CHAIN DRIVE Jet
Super-sonic type jet, delta-wing model. Realistic controls—simulated gauges. Chrome-plated spinner and intake, "jewel-like" reflector. Ball-bearing enclosed chain drive. Rubber block pedals. Ball-bearing 8-in. double-disc steel wheels. 1¾-in. rubber tires. Heavy gauge steel body. Stratosphere blue and rocket red baked-on enamel finish. By freight, express or truck. Wt. 38 lbs.
79 N M8967—45 in. long; 25-in. wingspread. . . $28.95

All Steel "Pedal-Drive" Autos

[E] "Super Sport"—the fashion car of the juvenile auto world. Newest bittersweet color, trim and wheels castle tan—lots of chrome. Ball-bearing wheels, drive mechanism. "Free steering." Heavy gauge steel body. Ball-bearing 8-in. double-disc steel wheels. 1-in. fancy-tread solid rubber tires. Rubber block pedals adjust. Seat pad. 39x17 inches wide.
79 N 08938L—Shpg. wt. 39 lbs. . . $21.98

[F] Ladder Fire Truck. Room for extra fireman. Hand rails, rear step, deck. Chrome-plated bell. Two removable wood ladders. Ball-bearing wheels, drive mechanism. "Free steering." Ball-bearing 8-in. double disc steel wheels. ⅝-in. solid rubber tires. Seat pad. Rubber block pedals adjust. Heavy gauge steel body. Red baked-on enamel finish; white trim. Size 47x17 in. Wt. 37 lbs.
79 N 08923L—Was $20.95 . . . . . $19.85

[G] Sleek Sport Car at a low price. Quick turning, easy pedaling. Full ball-bearing drive mechanism. 8-in. double-disc steel wheels. ⅝-in. solid rubber tires. Rubber block pedals adjust. Seat pad. Heavy gauge steel body, blue baked-on enamel finish; white, silver color trim. 36x17 in.
79 N 08910L—Shpg. wt. 28 lbs. . . $11.98

[H] Roy Rogers' "Nellybelle." Authentic reproduction of Roy's jeep . . . with extra play features. Tow hook—folding windshield—removable overhead rack—tail gate that opens—gun port—license plate. Heavy gauge steel. Ball-bearing rear axle for easy driving. Seat, solid rubber pedals adjust. 8-in. steel disc wheels. 1¾-in. semi-pneumatic rubber tires. Blue-gray baked-on enamel finish; white, red trim. 40¾ in. long.
79 N 08931L—Shipping weight 38 pounds. Was $22.95 . . . . $20.95

Catalog numbers with letter "M" as 79 N M8980 shipped by freight, express or truck.

270 . . SEARS, ROEBUCK AND CO.

This page of a 1954 Sears, Roebuck and Co. catalog shows a variety of pedal vehicles. Old store catalogs can be useful in the identification and restoration of pedal cars.

hood ornament, windshield, steering wheel, paint scheme, graphics, and other details can be determined from these catalog pictures. Also listed in the specifications was whether or not various trim pieces were plated or painted, which helps you determine the correct finish to use on each pedal car part. These catalogs may also serve to date your pedal car, as most manufacturers made subtle changes each year in their offerings. Since original pedal car catalogs are rare and expensive, copies are available from pedal car collectors and vendors (see directory at the back of this book).

Additional sources for pictures and information on pedal cars are old store catalogs. Montgomery Ward, Sears & Roebuck, F.A.O. Schwartz, Western Auto, and many other stores featured pedal cars in their catalogs. It can be challenging to find these old catalogs, but you may be able to find them through catalog collectors who advertise in national antique publications or at a paper collectibles show. Many old magazine ads and postcards featured pedal cars as well and these pictures may be helpful; however, they offer no specifications to assist you.

Attending a pedal car show is also a good way of obtaining information about your particular model. These shows feature original and restored pedal cars that you can photograph for reference or for your own enjoyment. Usually the owners are more than willing to talk about their car and can offer you some helpful advice. By subscribing to a pedal car newsletter you will be informed of most upcoming pedal car shows.

At a pedal car show a variety of children's vehicles are on display. Trophies are often presented to winners of certain categories such as best original or best of show. (Courtesy John Rastall)

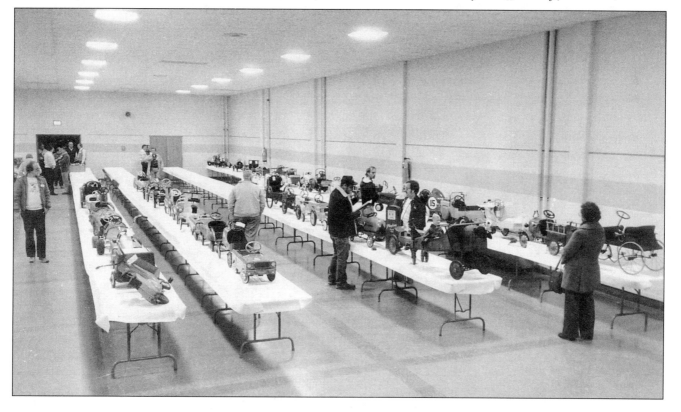

RESEARCH AND DOCUMENTATION

It is a good idea to photograph the original graphics. If not commercially available, the design should be copied using tracing paper and a pencil.

Networking with other pedal car collectors and restorers is another good method of obtaining information. Some vendors specialize in specific pedal cars and are very knowledgeable regarding particular models. Still other enthusiasts own or have owned different makes and models of pedal cars. Through networking with others, you can tap into a very valuable source of data that comes from the experience and knowledge that fellow collectors already possess. Instead of learning by trial and error, let others help you pave the way for a smooth restoration. To get in touch with other enthusiasts subscribe to a national magazine for pedal car collectors such as *Wheel Goods Trader*.

After completing some preliminary research on your pedal car you are ready to document the actual car as found. Take several photos of the pedal car from different angles. Natural light usually yields the best results so photograph your car outside. Don't forget to take a shot of the undercarriage and of any unusual graphics. Any areas that may be confusing to reassemble should be photographed so you will have a guide to assist you in reassembly. Having a few "before" photos displayed with your finished project is a good idea also—it illustrates your hard work at restoring the pedal car to like new condition.

If you don't have access to a camera, make a sketch of the car and jot down a few notes. If there are any original decals, emblems, or striping, take measurements to a reference point on the body so the new artwork can be placed in the exact location of the originals without any guesswork. Tracings of original graphics should also be done as an added precaution. Using tracing paper and a pencil, mark the outline of any graphics that are not available commercially. In this manner, a graphic artist could be employed to create a reasonable facsimile. If there are no remains of the original graphics, examine an old catalog illustration. An educated guess can be made as to

Be sure to determine the location of the graphics. This can be done by taking a measurement from the graphic to a reference point on the body. The distance from a body rivet to the front edge of the graphic will pinpoint the graphic's horizontal position.

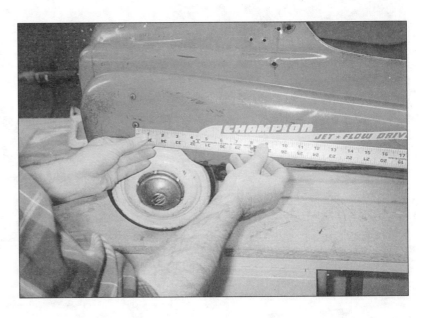

the placement of decals based on what the picture shows. Be sure to talk to other enthusiasts who may have restored a similar pedal car in the past, as they may be able to offer directions on the proper placement of graphics.

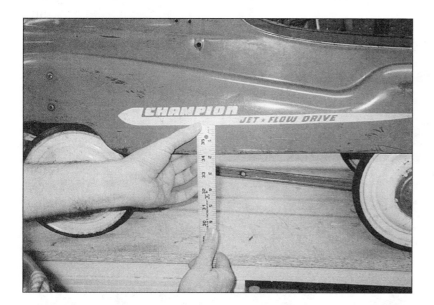

The measurement from the lower edge of the body to the lower edge of the graphic will allow you to place the graphic in the correct vertical position

It is not a good idea to rely solely on a photograph or catalog picture to capture the true original color of an old pedal car. It is better to find an area on the car that was protected from exposure, then clean it thoroughly and take it directly to the paint store for a color match. Good areas to look for covered original paint are underneath a piece of trim or beneath the undercarriage.

After completing the necessary research and documentation, you are ready to proceed with the next step in the restoration process—disassembly.

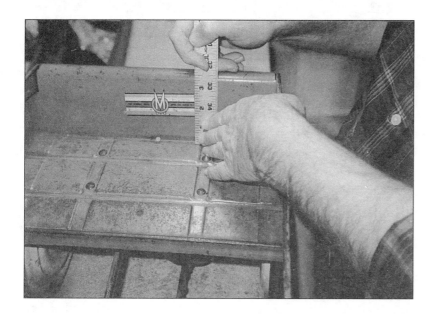

Placed slightly crooked at the factory, this Murray Ohio decal was centered on the seat back approximately 1-1/2 inches from the bottom edge of the seat. The new decal should be placed straight.

The project Champion after disassembly

CHAPTER 6

DISASSEMBLY AND PAINT MATCHING

DISASSEMBLY

Place the pedal car on a workbench or other suitable work surface at about waist height. This will save your back and make the disassembly process much more comfortable. Work in a well lit area within easy reach of any necessary tools. Begin by turning the car on its side to reveal any rusty fasteners. Spray all the fasteners with rust dissolver and let them soak for several minutes. This will give the rust dissolver time to do its work and allow the removal of screws and nuts that are heavily corroded. While spraying on the rust dissolver, examine the underside for any nonoriginal fasteners or holes. New fasteners will stand out due to their brighter plating and nonoriginal holes will usually have a tiny burr around the underside of the hole. Several nonoriginal fasteners and holes were found in the project Champion. Remember to place all original fasteners and other small parts that are removed in resealable plastic bags. This will prevent loss and allow for labeling of the bags if necessary.

Next, turn the car right side up and remove the hood ornament. Many hood ornaments are held on with screws or tabs or both. After removing the screws and straightening the tabs the hood ornament can be closely examined. Use great caution when straightening tabs of any kind, for they are often broken off by hasty restorers. Discoloration or worn off plating is normal and the piece can usually be replated without great expense; however, heavy pitting or corrosion will make the surface unacceptable for plating. Examination of the Champion hood ornament reveals it was heavily rusted and was painted over with silver paint to look more attractive to potential buyers, so it will not be a good candidate for replating. Fortunately, an excellent quality reproduction is available in chromium-plated stamped steel for a reasonable price. Save the original part, for it does have some value to a person who has an incomplete project car to sell. The hood ornament is a critical piece of trim and is often missing, but you needn't worry, as most hood ornaments for pedal cars are being reproduced.

The next part to be removed is the steering wheel. To remove the steering wheel, hold the outer rim with one hand and use an open end or socket wrench to loosen the nut. This particular steering wheel has a slot in the center hub that accepts the rectangular end of the steering shaft. This slot should be checked for excessive wear. If required, a small amount of metal could be welded in this area and the slot could be filed to its original shape. When checking the steering wheel for damage, make sure it hasn't been distorted. An acrylic hammer or rubber mallet may be used to "true up" the wheel. If the steering wheel is missing, as is very common with old pedal cars, don't be overly concerned. This particular steering wheel was used for many years on several different models of Murray Ohio pedal cars and used examples can be easily located. A fair quality reproduction is also available.

Next, remove the windshield by unscrewing two machine screws and nuts on each side of the car. Slide the tab out of the rectangular slot on the hood and lift the windshield from the body. With the windshield separated from the car, look it over carefully for any damage or twisting to its shape. If it is distorted, gently bend it into the proper shape. If the edges are bent, use a pair of duckbill pliers to straighten out the area. It is important to try to fix the windshield since reproductions vary in quality and are expensive. Don't feel too bad though if your particular pedal car is missing its windshield. Pedal car parts manufacturers realize that these items are usually missing or damaged and have reproduced many styles to fit all types of pedal cars.

Proceed to remove any other fasteners that are accessible while the car is in an upright position. On the front bumper of the Champion two truss head screws with square nuts secure the front end braces to the body. Use a standard screwdriver and pliers to remove these fasteners. Four truss head screws backed by square nuts hold the rear axle assembly to the underside of the seat. Once again, remove these fasteners using a standard screwdriver and pliers.

Sometimes this screw and nut combination will not loosen even with rust dissolver. Over time the screw heads may be stripped and the corners of the nuts may be rounded. To facilitate their removal, use a rotary tool with a special cut-off wheel. It is recommended that the rotary tool be operated at high speed (20,000-30,000 rpm) using a 1-1/4-inch composite cut-off wheel with reinforcing mesh. Begin by cutting the screw shaft flush with the top of the nut. Next make a cut that bisects the nut through its center. When the cut is nearly through, shut off the rotary tool and use a screwdriver to pry apart the two halves of the nut. The nut will break away easily, allowing the screw to be taken out. This method allows rusty or stripped fasteners to be safely removed without risking damage to the surrounding sheet metal.

Next, turn the pedal car on its side and separate the rear axle assembly from the body. It will be necessary to remove the pedals in order to completely remove the drivetrain. Begin by using a pair of needlenose pliers to straighten the cotter pin that holds the pedal in place. Pull the cotter pin completely out of the hole in the pedal rod and slide off the retaining washer. The pedal can now be removed, followed by the connecting strap that is attached to the rear axle.

Now that the rear axle assembly is no longer attached to the body the wheels can be removed. Murray often used a number of metal tabs to hold hubcaps in place. To remove a hubcap, use a standard screwdriver to bend the tabs away from the hubcap, taking extra caution not to break off the tabs. Now pry up on the hubcap and remove it from the wheel. On most pedal cars, as on full-size cars, the hubcaps or wheel covers hide the fasteners that hold the wheel to the axle. On pedal cars one of the rear wheels is usually free wheeling, which is to say that the wheel itself is not directly secured to the axle. The other wheel is known as the drive wheel and usually has a slot in it to accommodate the slotted end of the axle, which is threaded to accept a nut. When the drive wheel is slid on the threaded end of the axle and the nut is tightened, the axle and drive wheel will move as one unit. This allows the transfer of power from the pedals through the drivetrain to the drive wheel.

To remove the free wheel, use needlenose pliers to pull the cotter pin from the axle, then slide off the wheel. On each side of the wheel there is usually a washer that should be saved. In order to remove the drive wheel it will be necessary to loosen the nut that secures the wheel to the threaded end of the axle. Do this with an open end or socket wrench. When the nut has been removed, the wheel can be slid off the axle. Now is a good time to completely inspect the rear axle assembly for any stress cracks, bad bearings, or damage to the threaded end of the axle. If needed, use the proper size die to recut worn or damaged threads on the axle. You will find that the underside of the axle assembly is an excellent spot to find an area of the original paint that was protected from the elements. This area can be used to obtain a color match for refinishing purposes.

With the rear axle assembly completely removed and disassembled, you may concentrate on the steering assembly. Begin by prying up the tabs on the front wheels and removing the hubcaps. Since both front wheels are free wheeling, merely remove the cotter pins and slide off the wheels. Next remove the two cotter pins that hold the steering shaft in place and slide the steering shaft out. Inspect the threaded end of the steering shaft for any worn or damaged threads and use the proper size die to recut the threads if necessary. Then remove the two machine screws and square nuts that secure the steering assembly to the front support. The front support provides a framework for the front spindles, pedal rods, and steering shaft. This part is riveted to the body and should only be removed if it will interfere with any body work. If the front support is removed, body work should be completed and the part reriveted before the final finish is applied. If riveting is not practical, an alternative is to use "fake rivets" during reassembly. "Fake rivets" have a head that resembles a rivet and a threaded shaft to accommodate a nut. When a painted or plated part is assembled with these type of fasteners there is virtually no risk of damaging the finish.

After the steering assembly is removed from the pedal car, inspect it for damage. Make sure the steering mechanism can move back and forth freely. At this point, all parts have been removed from the pedal car body and you may now proceed to remove the old, worn out tire rubber from the wheels.

After many years of hard use, the tires will certainly need to be replaced and the wheels will need to be repainted. In order to separate the tire from the wheel it will be necessary to cut the tire with a pair of sidecutters. This will take effort since a piece of wire runs through the tire, but when this is accomplished it will be easy to peel the tire away from the wheel. The tire itself is actually a type of thick-walled, extruded rubber hose. One method that pedal car manufacturers used to apply the tire was the following: First, the tire rubber was cut to the proper length, then a slightly longer piece of wire was passed through the center of the "tire." The rubber and wire were then wrapped around the outside of the wheel and a tire machine spread apart the rubber so the two ends of the wire could be twisted together. After the wire was trimmed, the rubber was released to cover the joined ends of the wire. If done properly, the rubber would meet tightly and a seam was hardly noticeable. The result was a rubber tire that was held in place by a strong wire. This type of installation proved to be very durable and stood up to many years of hard use.

Once the tires are removed from the wheels, check the wheels for any damage to the edges of the rims. Inspect the drive wheel and check for excessive wear to the slot. Don't forget to assess the condition of the hubcaps. The plating on the hubcaps of most old pedal cars will have deteriorated, so plan on having these parts replated at a reputable plating shop. If the hubcaps are dented or heavily pitted you may want to purchase a set of reproduced wheel covers. In the case of the Champion, the hubcaps were severely dented and had deep scratches that could not be polished out; therefore, a high quality set of reproduction hubcaps were ordered.

Only now that the project has been completely disassembled and all the parts have been thoroughly inspected do you see the true picture of the overall condition. Don't be too upset if a few bad surprises are discovered at this stage. It is better that these problems surface now when they can be dealt with easily. After completing several steps in the restoration process it may be difficult to go back and correct a preexisting condition. With the pedal car apart, you may be hasty to begin reconditioning the various parts; however, now will be the only chance to obtain a sample of the original paint from an unexposed part of the pedal car, which brings the project into the next phase—matching the original paint.

1. Pedal car disassembly is much easier when done in an organized and well lit workshop.

2. To begin the dirty work of disassembly, turn the car on its side.

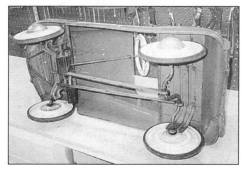

3. Spray all the fasteners with rust dissolver.

4. Use a slotted screwdriver to remove the machine screw that holds the hood ornament in place (right). It will be necessary to straighten the two tabs that hold the tail of the ornament to the hood.

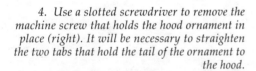

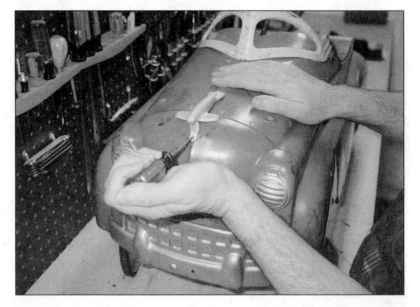

5. This particular hood ornament is in the shape of an airplane and mimics those found on full-size cars of the 1950s. Once the hood ornament has been removed, it can be inspected for damage. This one is badly pitted and would require the services of a custom plater, which can be very costly. Since an excellent quality reproduction ornament is available, the original ornament will not be used.

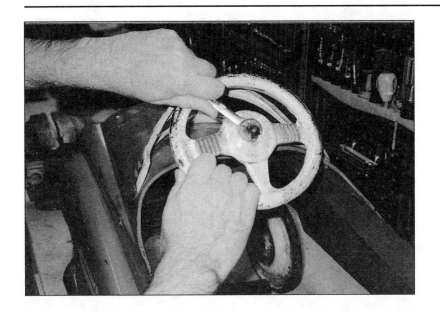

6. *To remove the steering wheel, grasp it firmly with one hand and use a 9/16-inch open end wrench to remove the steering wheel nut.*

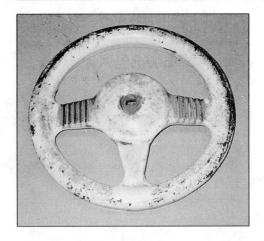

7. With the steering wheel off, check for any distortion by placing the wheel on a flat surface. If distorted, use an acrylic hammer to return the wheel to its original shape. Be sure to examine both the top and bottom for any damage.

8. Remove the two screws and nuts that hold the windshield in place.

9. After straightening the tab from underneath the hood, the windshield can be lifted off the body.

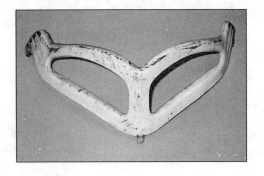

10. With the windshield separated from the body, check for any distortion, stress cracks, or edge damage.

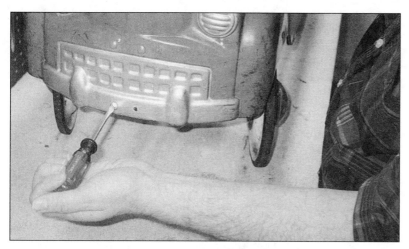

11. *Remove the two screws that secure the front end brace to the front bumper.*

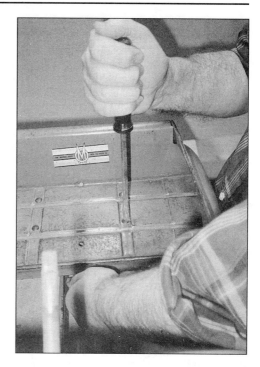

12. *Loosen the four screws that hold the rear axle assembly to the underside of the seat.*

13. *On occasion, old fasteners may require extra measures to remove. Using the rotary tool, cut off the screw end flush with the top of the nut.*

14. *Turn the cut-off wheel vertically and begin to cut through the middle of the nut.*

15. When the cut is nearly through, stop the rotary tool.

16. Insert a slotted screwdriver into the cut and pry apart the nut.

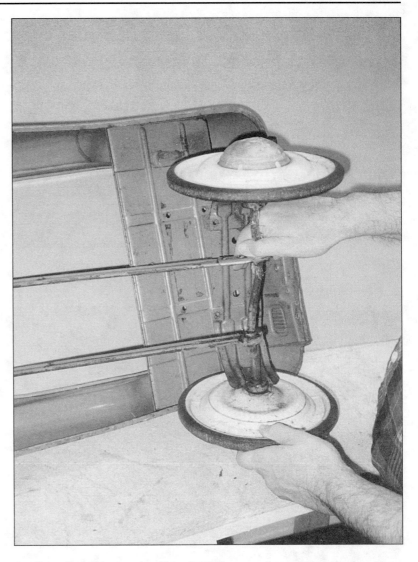

17. Turn the pedal car on its side and pull the rear axle assembly away from the body.

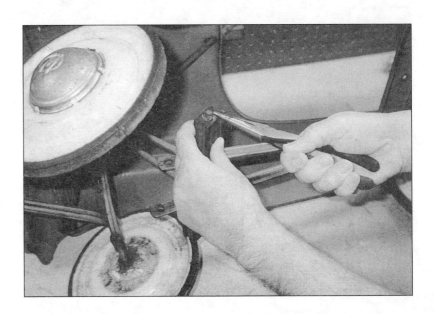

18. Using a pair of needlenose pliers, remove the cotter pin that holds the pedal in place.

19. Slide off the retaining washer and the pedal.

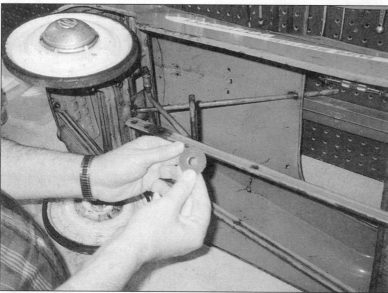

20. To free the strut from the pedal rod, slide the strut completely off.

21. These pedals show heavy wear and are no longer pliable; they should be replaced. The large washers are not original and will not be reused.

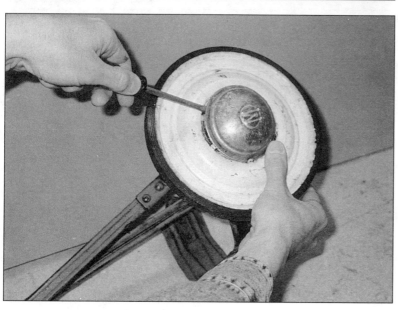

22. With the rear axle assembly completely free of the body, the rear wheels can now be removed. Gently pry up the six tabs that hold the hubcap in place and lift the hubcap using a standard screwdriver.

DISASSEMBLY AND PAINT MATCHING

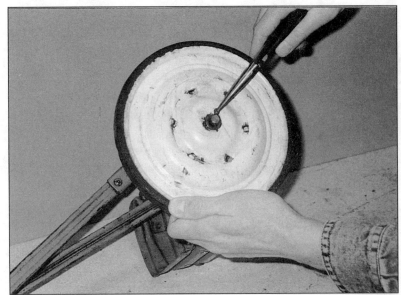

23. On the free wheel side of the axle, use needlenose pliers to extract the cotter pin, then simply slide the wheel off.

24. On the drive wheel, hold the wheel firmly and loosen the wheel nut with an open end wrench.

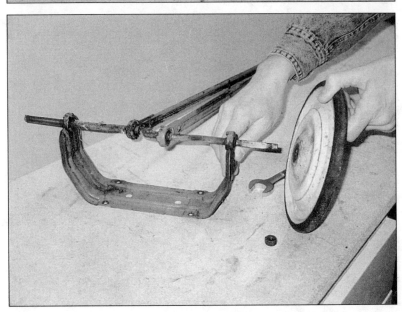

25. Slide the drive wheel off the axle.

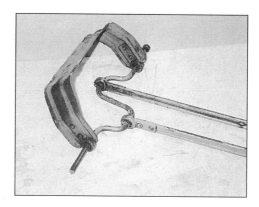

26. *The rear axle assembly as removed from the Champion. Check for any stress cracks or damage to the bearings. Be sure to place the drive wheel nut back onto the axle so as not to lose it.*

27. *Begin the removal of the front wheels by prying up the tabs and hubcap.*

28. *Straighten and pull the cotter pin using needlenose pliers. Remove the washer and slide the wheel off the axle.*

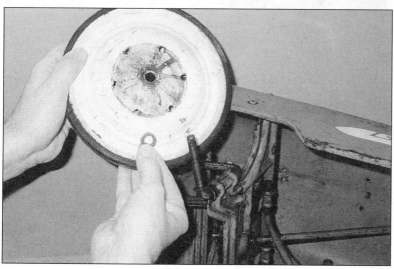

134

29. Using a standard screwdriver and pliers, remove the two machine screws and square nuts that secure the front steering assembly in place.

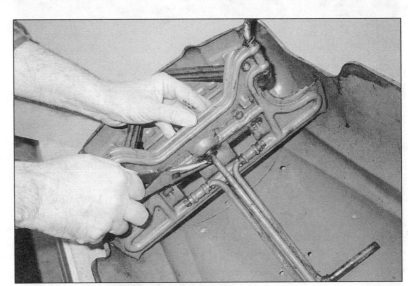

30. Remove the cotter pin that retains the steering shaft near the top of the front axle assembly.

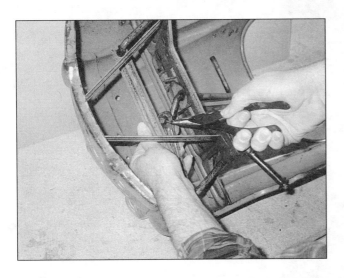
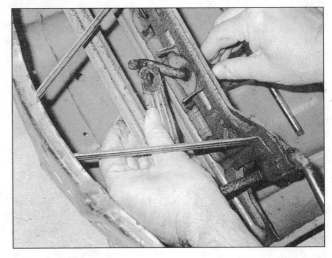

31. Remove the cotter pin that attaches the steering shaft to the steering link and separate the two components.

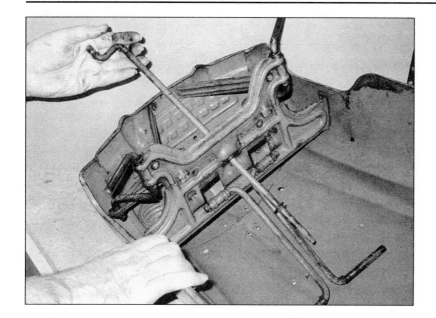

32. Slide the steering shaft out of the front axle assembly.

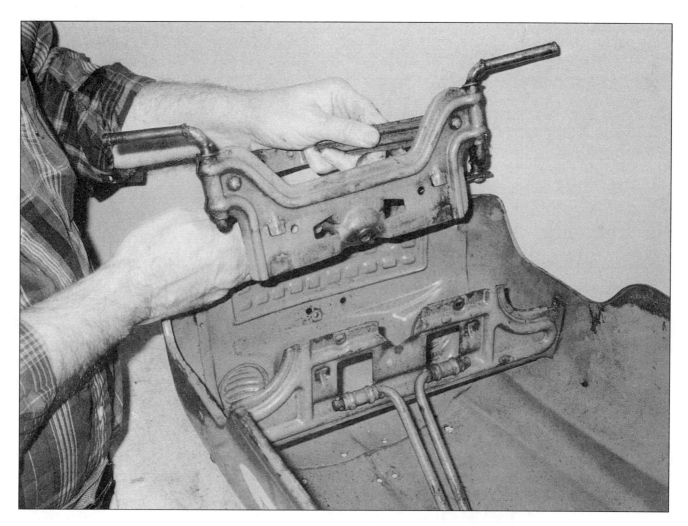

33. Pry the front steering assembly up and out of the front undercarriage. Since these parts fit together snugly, it may require some extra effort to separate them.

34. Using sidecutters, cut through the tire and peel it away from the wheel. A length of wire runs through the tire, making it tough to slice.

35. The Champion's hubcaps have numerous abrasions and dents, making replating very costly. Since a fine quality reproduction is available for a reasonable price, these hubcaps will not be reused.

36. It is a good practice to place all the old fasteners in a resealable plastic bag. In this manner they won't get lost and can be located easily when selecting replacement fasteners.

PAINT MATCHING

Over the years, a pedal car's once brilliant and colorful finish may degrade to a dull and lifeless surface. Fortunately, while disassembling a pedal car you will discover areas that have been protected from the elements. These areas may lie underneath a piece of trim like a hood ornament or headlight pod or beneath sections of the undercarriage. You want to find a representative spot of original paint so you can use it to obtain a new mixture of that exact color. On the project Champion an area of well-preserved paint was found underneath the rear axle assembly. This area was a bright medium blue and looked far more appealing than the faded exterior of the Champion. The next step was to take this part directly to the paint store for a color match.

When the term "paint store" is used, it means a store that specializes in automotive finishes and supplies. Bringing a part directly to the paint store will allow a paint technician to match the color. Many home improvement stores have a special machine that can match any color of house paint by placing a sample under the device. Stores that deal in automotive finishes, however, still use the old-fashioned method: the human eye. Through a small series of trial and error formulas, the correct color of paint can be obtained from a sample color.

The paint technician first selects a base color to tint, then colors are added to bring the mixture into the same color range as that of the sample. Next the technician fine tunes the mixture by adding a small amount of color and dabbing the newly created mixture on top of the sample. This process may be repeated several times until the color is right. An experienced paint formulator can rival computer color matching and will even take into account any shade changes that might occur when the paint has completely dried.

Regarding the Champion, the formulator quickly brought the paint mixture into the basic realm of blue that was on the sample. A tinge of green was necessary to correct the shade. After several dabs of the finger and tiny additions of color the mixture was ready, and when placed side-by-side with the original blue color of the sample it was a perfect match. A quart of fresh acrylic enamel in this medium blue color was obtained for use on the project Champion.

Now attention was focused on the white paint for the windshield, steering wheel, and wheels. An area underneath the hubcaps on the wheels had some protected white paint. The paint technician examined this area and performed a color match, for some shades of white, such as a bright white, would have been inappropriate for use on this project.

The last color of paint to be chosen was the silver for the grille and headlights. Since these areas on the Champion were faded, the silver was matched from a well-preserved and similar model of Murray pedal car. Since only a small amount of

A good spot to look for original paint that hasn't faded over the years is underneath the rear axle hanger

paint was required, a medium silver was selected in the form of a spray can. While at the paint store you may want to purchase all the necessary supplies for applying the finish to the pedal car. Detailed information on painting pedal cars may be found in the chapter entitled "Paint Application."

After returning from the paint store with the properly matched colors of paint, you are ready to begin the next phase of the project—paint and rust removal on all parts of the disassembled pedal car.

Formulator Thomas Schramm of the Model Paint Company begins color matching by selecting the proper base

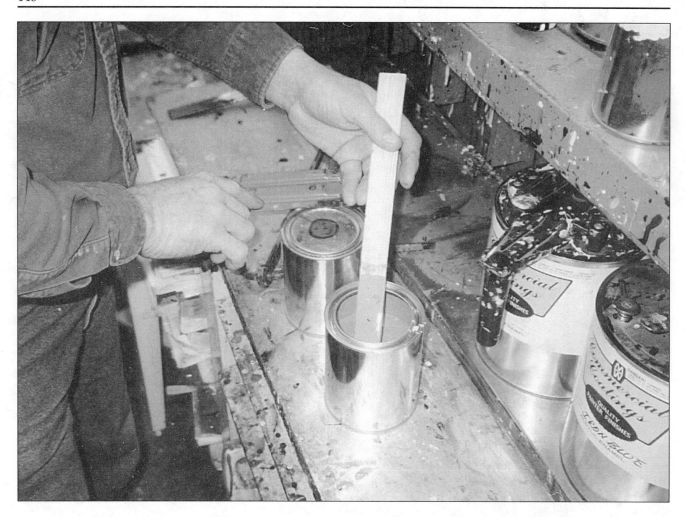

Small amounts of tints are added to the base, and after each addition the formulator dabs a spot on the original color

When just the right amount of tints are added, the new paint matches the original color exactly

The new blue paint for the Champion is sealed and agitated in a paint mixer

Acrylic enamel was chosen for its durability. One quart each of blue and white paint will be sufficient for the pedal car.

The disassembled pedal car gleaming of bare metal after its trip to the commercial stripper

CHAPTER 7

RUST AND PAINT REMOVAL

At this point the pedal car is completely apart, yet hardly ready to accept any type of finish. Most restorers understand that it is not acceptable to paint over rust, dents, or damaged paint. This would produce very shoddy results and maybe a few laughs from fellow enthusiasts; therefore, it is critical that all parts be stripped down to bare metal. Bare metal is the best surface to start any repairs and allows you to discover any hidden defects, such as stress cracks or defective welds. In order to remove all traces of rust and old paint from the pedal car and return it to bare metal, several methods can be used.

1. SANDING AND GRINDING: The use of sandpaper for paint removal is slow and tedious work, even with an electric sander. Air-powered sanders work the best, yet most sanding methods are ineffective on irregular or hard to reach surfaces and deeply rusted areas. A handheld electric or air-powered grinder could be used to grind away rust, but unfortunately grinders leave deep scratches that will require additional amounts of fillers to even out the surface.

2. HEAT GUN: Using a heat gun to remove paint from a pedal car is another method that can be employed. A heat gun is a small device consisting of a heating element and a fan. When the heating element gets hot, a fan blows a stream of air over the element. The hot air stream can be directed over a painted surface, causing the paint to loosen its bond with the material underneath. Before beginning work with the heat gun, make sure the work area is well-ventilated and the operator is wearing a respirator. This is necessary because the heated paint will give off fumes. With the heat gun about one inch away, aim the nozzle at the painted surface. After a few seconds the paint will began to change color and may bubble up. Have a scraper handy and proceed to scrape away the old paint. Don't try to rush to do the whole project at once; it is better to completely clean a small area before moving on to the next section. This method is slow and tedious and produces a lot of nasty paint fumes. Caution must be taken to let the heat gun cool thoroughly before storing.

3. SANDBLASTING AND GLASSBEADING: Many restorers like to use sandblasting or glassbeading to remove old paint and rust. Sandblasting involves cleaning a metal surface by spraying it with a high velocity stream of air containing sand particles. Glassbeading is similar except the abrasive used is fine particles of glass. Usually the setup involves a reservoir or tank to hold the sand or glass beads, an air compressor to provide pressure, and a hose with a nozzle to direct the stream. These types of freestanding units are portable and require the operator to wear a hood to protect the face and eyes from flying abrasives.

An alternative is to use a sandblasting cabinet. Sandblasting cabinets are self-contained units that allow the operator to place a part inside the cabinet. When a part is placed into the cabinet and the door is closed, the sandblasting may begin. The operator looks through a window and, using a pair of rubber gloves that protrudes into the cabinet, can manipulate the part under a high-speed sand/air mixture. All sandblasters require an adequate compressor capacity. If a compressor's capacity is too small, it will starve the nozzle and reduce the effectiveness of the sandblaster. In addition, a good sandblasting setup will have an in-line air filter/moisture separator to filter excess humidity from the incoming air supply.

Sandblasting can remove rust and old paint more effectively than sanding or grinding; however, there are a few drawbacks to sandblasting pedal cars. First, sandblasting alters the surface of the metal. It causes the surface texture of the metal to become rough, much like sandpaper. When it comes time to prime and paint a sandblasted surface, extra layers of primer/filler have to be used to help smooth out the roughness. Secondly, if a cabinet is not used, sandblasting is extremely messy. A fine coating of sand-like dust will descend on everything in the work area. If you decide to use the same area for painting, it must be free of grit and sand that could contaminate the paint job. Finally, the pedal car parts themselves can trap grit and sand in bearings, wheels, and undercarriage components. If these contaminates are not removed, they may find their way into the finished painted surface. Sand might even get into the pedaling or steering mechanism, causing a gritty sound when these components are actuated.

4. CHEMICAL PAINT STRIPPERS AND RUST REMOVERS: The use of store bought chemicals to strip paint and remove rust is another alternative for you to consider. Usually these products contain caustic agents that attack the chemical makeup of the paint or oxidized areas of metal. Since these products are highly irritating to the skin, you will need protective clothing such as coveralls, gloves, goggles, and a respirator.

This pressure type sandblaster is portable and holds 65 lbs. of abrasive. When using a 1/8-inch nozzle, a 3 H.P. air compressor that can provide 15 CFM at 80 PSI is required.

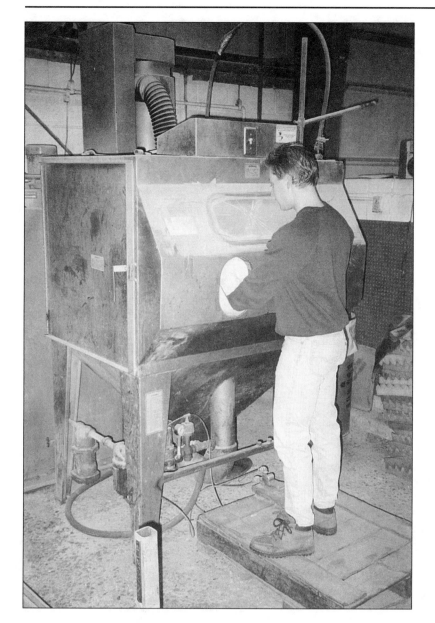

A sandblasting cabinet can be used to remove rust and paint from metal parts. Since the unit is self-contained, sand particles are confined to the inside of the cabinet.

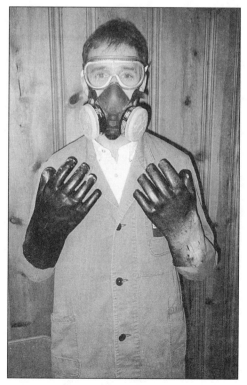

Before using any type of caustic paint or rust removers, the restorer should don protective clothing

To strip a pedal car body, place the project in a well-ventilated area and apply the chemical stripper with a brush. After a few minutes the paint will "crinkle" and can be taken off using a scraper or coarse steel wool. Unfortunately, if there are several coats of old paint it will be necessary to apply more than one coat of paint remover. Stripping the paint from the underside of the pedal car is difficult also. Some areas such as inside corners may be difficult to reach. When all the paint has been stripped, the pedal car must be washed thoroughly with detergent and water to remove any traces of chemicals.

Using chemical strippers to remove paint and rust from pedal cars in the home workshop is a time consuming and messy job. If you choose this method, it is recommended you purchase an aircraft coating remover from a specialty paint store and work outside with full protective clothing. This type

RUST AND PAINT REMOVAL

To apply a chemical paint stripper, brush on the product and allow a few minutes for a reaction to occur. Coarse steel wool or a scraper may be used to rid the surface of any old paint. Several applications may be necessary.

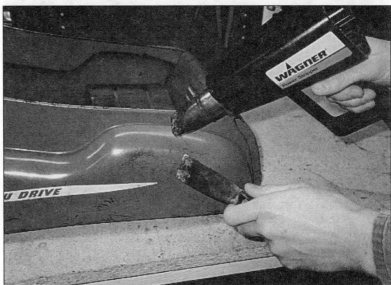

To use the heat gun to remove paint, hold the nozzle about one inch from the surface. After several seconds use the scraper to peel up the old paint. Work a small section at a time rather than trying to do a large area all at once.

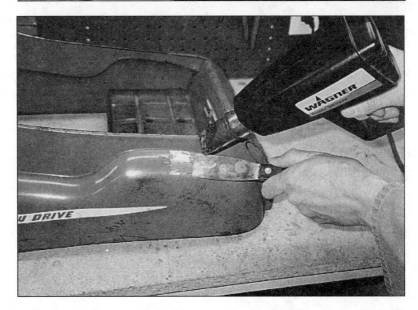

of stripper is more effective on paint than what is offered at most local hardware stores.

Other products such as nontoxic strippers containing citrus additives are very slow to react and still require several applications to work adequately. Rust converters should not be used, as these products do not actually remove rust, they merely cover it up.

Aircraft coating remover is superior to ordinary paint strippers

COMMERCIAL CHEMICAL STRIPPING OPERATIONS

Some restorers feel there is a lot of surface area to strip on a pedal car, but think for a moment on how much work would be involved in stripping hundreds, even thousands of automotive parts for GM, Ford, and Chrysler. That is a typical workload for a commercial paint stripping operation. During assembly line painting operations at a major automotive plant, something occasionally goes wrong, resulting in a batch of parts with a poor paint job. To remedy this situation the automotive company sends these parts to a commercial paint stripper, which, through a series of processes, strips the parts back to clean bare metal. The parts are then sent back to the automotive plant where they can be refinished.

The big three automotive companies are not the only ones who can benefit from the services of a commercial paint stripper. Pedal car restorers can utilize these services at a very reasonable cost. Besides being affordable, a commercial stripper saves you time, energy, aggravation, and exposure to hazardous chemicals. The best part is that the final result is superior to any other method of paint and rust removal. An important consideration to note is that this process was designed mainly for iron and steel. Pot metal will not fare well in the process and should be stripped using other methods.

In order to understand how the process works, let's follow the Champion pedal car on its journey through International Paint Stripping of Romulus, Michigan, a commercial stripping operation. Before the pedal car body and parts were taken to the stripper, the parts were wired together to prevent them from getting lost. Upon arriving at the commercial stripper, a tag was obtained from the office to identify the Champion parts. The parts were then placed inside a pyrolytic oven and were heated to approximately eight hundred degrees Fahrenheit. A pyrolytic oven is specially designed to burn off paint from metal parts. When the oven was turned off and had cooled down, the parts were removed. Only a microscopic layer of ash remained on the disassembled Champion, for all the paint had been completely and uniformly burned off.

At this point the pedal car was placed inside a large metal basket attached to an overhead crane. A technician then lowered the basket and its contents into a large tank of hydroclhoric acid. The parts had to remain submerged in the acid

RUST AND PAINT REMOVAL

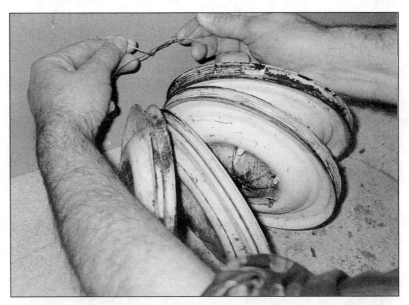

Before parts are dropped off at a commercial paint stripper, they should be wired together to prevent being lost

The pedal car and parts are placed inside a pyrolytic oven by International Paint Stripping manager Mark Kochanoski. Reaching eight hundred degrees Fahrenheit, the oven's heat will burn off any old paint.

When the oven has cooled down the parts can be removed. With all the old paint burned off, only a light ash residue is left on the parts.

The parts are then placed in a large, metal basket. A technician for IPS, Cliff Hutchins, then lowers the parts into a tank of acid.

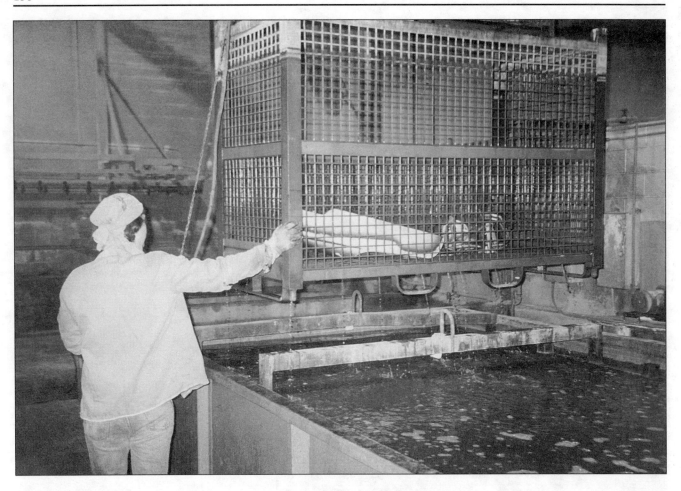

After remaining in the acid bath for several minutes, the parts are lifted out and drained

bath for several minutes. When the parts were raised out of the acid, the gleam of bare metal could be seen. The pedal car was then removed from the basket and rinsed with water sprayed from a powerwash wand. As a final step, the bare metal parts can be sprayed with an oil coating to retard oxidation.

As previously stated, this process is for iron and steel. Some pedal vehicles, such as pedal tractors made by Eska in the 1950s, were made of cast aluminum. IPS has a special process to strip aluminum. Aluminum parts are not placed in an oven because the high temperatures could melt the aluminum; instead, aluminum parts are lowered into a molten salt unit where paint will separate from the parts without harming the aluminum.

As a final step, IPS employee Ed Williams rinses the parts with a powerwash

Aluminum parts such as early Eska pedal tractors may be stripped in a molten salt unit

A pedal car show is a good place to look for parts

CHAPTER 8

PARTS ACQUISITION AND PLATING

PARTS ACQUISITION: ORIGINAL VS. REPRODUCTION

Obtaining parts to complete a pedal car is actually a floating step in the restoration process. That is to say some parts may be located or ordered when the pedal car is first purchased and other parts may be harder to find and you will have to pursue several leads over a period of time. A good practice is to wait until the pedal car is completely disassembled and you have assessed the condition of all existing parts before seeking replacements.

In the case of the project Champion, several parts needed replacing. These parts included the pedals, hubcaps, hood ornament, graphics, and tire rubber. After reviewing the sources for parts it was determined that the pedals, hubcaps, and hood ornament would be ordered from Pedal Car Accessory's of Pomona, California. The owner, Van Eden, has a good reputation for offering quality parts at a reasonable price. When the parts arrived, they were all top quality and matched the original parts exactly.

Graphics were ordered from Pedal Car Graphics, which operates out of Taylors, South Carolina. This company has an excellent track record of serving the needs of the pedal car restorer. Bob Ellsworth, the owner, was glad to provide the Champion graphics as well as the Murray Ohio seat label. Bulk tire rubber was bought from Portell Restorations of Hematite, Missouri. As a favor, owner Dan Portell agreed to sell just enough rubber to make four tires.

Some restorers insist on using only original parts. This is fine; however, many parts vendors are producing fine quality reproductions that are exactly like the originals. As a general rule, use the original parts if they can be refinished. If not, seek out other original parts and if still unsuccessful, use excellent quality reproductions. Most restorers know that in order to find pedal car parts such as rubber goods and hubcaps in new condition, they will most likely have to purchase these items as reproductions. No restorer wants to start working on a pedal car and then find out that the proper parts required to finish the project are unavailable. Fortunately, today's pedal car restorers have several options on how to locate pedal car parts.

PARTS VENDORS

One of the easiest and most convenient methods of locating parts is to contact a pedal car parts vendor. Pedal car parts vendors provide reproduction parts that are generally of good quality. Some parts are being made one at a time in a small job shop in the U.S.; other parts are being mass produced in a sweat shop overseas. This is one reason for the price and quality differences that can occur in the pedal car parts market. Beware of parts that require heavy modifications—they may end up forcing you to invest a ridiculous amount of time and money.

Some parts vendors have a limited supply of original or N.O.S. (new old stock) parts. Generally, original parts are difficult to locate and thus expensive to purchase. Don't be discouraged if a few original parts cannot be located for your pedal car. Use good quality reproduction parts and the restoration will turn out fine. For a list of pedal car parts vendors please see the directory in the back of this book.

It is also prudent to have a general idea of what parts are and are not available. Below is a general list of parts that are available.

General List of Available Pedal Car Parts

Steering wheels:	American National 7-1/2-inch
	Garton 7-1/2-inch
	Steelcraft 7-1/2-inch
	Murray Ohio
	AMF
Wheels:	American National 12-inch
	Rolls-auto
	Gendron 10-inch
	Toledo 10-inch
	Steelcraft 10-inch
	Murray "artillery"
	Murray "beehive"
	Murray 8-1/2-inch
	Murray 7-inch
	Garton
	BMC
Tires:	Available to fit most makes and models

Hubcaps:
American National 1-3/4-inch
American National 1-15/16-inch
Rolls-auto
Garton 3-1/4-inch
Garton 2-inch
Steelcraft 2-3/16-inch
Steelcraft 3-inch
Steelcraft octagonal
Murray "beehive" 3-inch
Murray/Steelcraft 3-5/8-inch
Murray/Steelcraft 4-inch
BMC
AMF

Windshields:
American National
Steelcraft
Garton
Murray
BMC
AMF

Lamps:
American National
Steelcraft
Gendron
Garton

Fenders:
American National
Steelcraft
Gendron

Bumpers:
American National
Steelcraft
Garton

Hood Ornaments: Most makes and models

Pedals: Available to fit most makes and models

Miscellaneous:
Bells
Sirens
Beacons
Ladders
Seat pads
Mirrors
Horns
Oil cans
Smoke stacks
Boat motors
Antennas
Trunk lids
Hose reels
Wrecker booms

PARTS ACQUISITION AND PLATING

Graphics (Available Through Bob Ellsworth)

Murray "City Fire Dept."
Champion
Station Wagon
Comet
Fire Car
Pontiac "City Fire Dept."
Fire Truck – Pump 1, Pump 2
BMC Fire Dept.
Checker Cab
AMF Fire Chief 503
Pinto
Cola-Cola Car
Dump Trac Trailer
Torpedo
Dump Truck
Hydraulic Dump Truck
Radio Sports Car
Maverick
Air Force Jeep
Police Sergeant Car
Police Chief
Pontiac Station Wagon
Police Radio Patrol
Police Radar Patrol
Fire Patrol
Good Humor Cycle
U.S. Army Command Car
Fire Chief (early 1960s)
Pontiac Fire Chief
Camaro
Skylark
Probe 3
AMF Super Jet Car
Fire Truck Engine No. 1
BMC Pacesetter Convertible
Super Sport
BMC Tractor Junior
R.A.F. Spitfire Plane
U.S. Army Pursuit Plane
U.S. Navy Pursuit Plane
Army Scout Plane
BMC Jet Ace
AMF Jet Sweep
Garton Fire Chief
Super-Sonda
Speedway Pace Car
Murray Diesel Tractor
Murray Trac Tractor

Ranch Trac Tractor
Tee Bird
Kidillac
Kidillac Police Chief
Kidillac Fire Chief
Police Hot Rod
Fire Chief Hot Rod
Casey Jones Locomotive
Casey Jones Coal Tender
Hot Rod
Chrysler Air Flow
U-Haul Trailer
AMF Rebel
Jolly Roger Boat
Skipper
Dolphin
Lancer
Tin Lizzie
Nellybelle Jeep
Royal Deluxe
Chrysler Fire Chief
Buick Fire Chief
Atomic Missile Plane
Super Sonic Jet
Fire Chief Battalion Car
Chrysler
Ranch Wagon
GTO
Gilmore Speedway Special
Happi Time Hawk
Garton Mark V
Garton Fire Chief
Garton Fire Truck
GTX
BMC Racer
Hook & Ladder 519
Fire Chief 512
AMF Fire Fighter 508
Fire Chief #611
AMF Transport
Highway Patrol
Dude Wagon
Tot Rod
Circus Car
Deluxe Fire Chief Auto
AMF Tote All
BMC Thunderbolt Senior

Available Pedal Tractor Parts to Fit Most Eska Tractors

Steering wheels
Rims
Hubcaps
Tires
Seats
Grilles (limited selection)
Chains

Pedals
Pedal shafts
Drawbars
Hitchpins
Shift levers
Noise makers
Decal sets

PEDAL CAR SHOWS

Another way to obtain pedal car parts is by attending a pedal car show. Throughout the country at different times during the year, one can almost always find a pedal car show. Sometimes held in conjunction with toy or advertising shows, pedal car shows are usually much anticipated and well-attended events. One advantage of attending a pedal car show is that you can barter the price of parts face to face with the seller, which sometimes results in a price reduction for the desired parts. You can also see and handle the part before making a purchase.

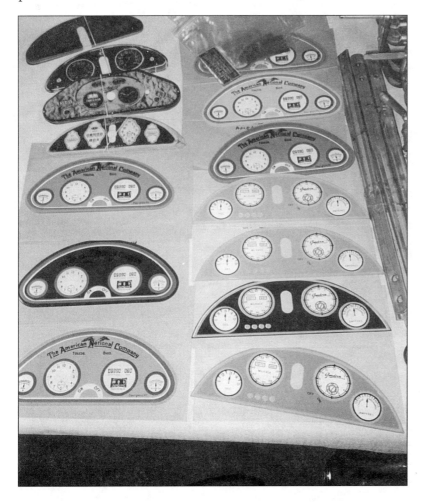

These instrument panel graphics were only a few of the many offerings at a recent pedal car show in Kalamazoo, MI

PARTS ACQUISITION AND PLATING

WANTED

Desperately need 2 front wheels and 4 hubcaps for 1950s Midwest Studebaker pedal car. Wheels are 6-1/4" in diameter. Hubcaps have "MID" stamped in center.

Taking out a classified ad in a national pedal car magazine is a good way to network for parts (Courtesy Wheel Goods Trader)

WANT ADS

As an additional option you may want to run a want ad seeking specific parts in a national pedal car magazine. In this manner, collectors and enthusiasts from around the country will have a chance to respond to the advertisement. Ads of this nature are generally inexpensive and eliminate a great deal of aggravation and footwork.

FASTENERS

An important aspect of parts acquisition is obtaining the proper fasteners. More often than not the original fasteners that held the pedal car together were stripped or rusted beyond repair. A simple trip to the local hardware store will not always yield the types of fasteners that a pedal car restorer will require. Therefore, you will need to visit a fastener store. Fastener stores (you can find them in your yellow pages) sell more than just nuts and bolts; a variety of fasteners in all shapes and sizes can be found there. When visiting a fastener store, be sure to bring the old fastener, even if damaged, to use as an example. Fastener store employees are generally very knowledgeable and are adept at gauging sizes and thread diameters. For the project Champion, fasteners were supplied by the knowledgeable and courteous folks at C & J Fastener in Redford, Michigan.

A trip to the fastener store will yield the best selection of fasteners to complete a pedal car restoration

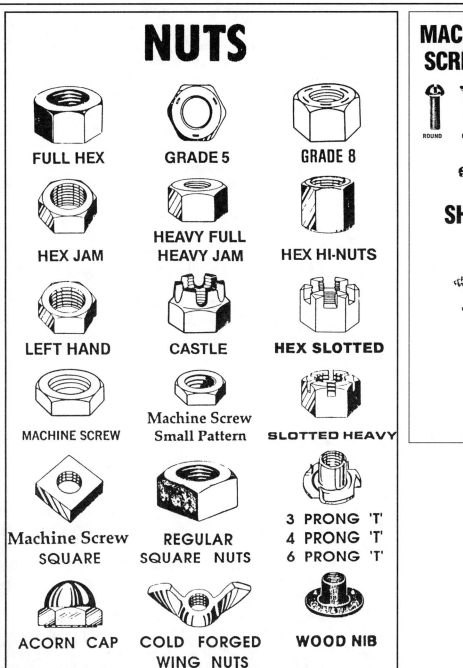

PLATING

One of the most noticeable and important aspects of restoring a pedal car is returning the trim back to its original luster. Brightwork such as hood ornaments, hubcaps, light bezels, and emblems are subject to corrosion and can appear dull over time. An amateur restorer might try to paint the parts silver in an attempt to make them presentable. Unfortunately, this method can never duplicate the beautiful shine that was on the part originally.

Another method that has been used is to place a thin layer of silver foil over the old part. In order to make the foil stick, the part is first covered with a spray adhesive. This method has been made popular by clay modelers who cover the trim parts of automotive mock-ups with foil. When the foil layer is smoothed over the surface it gives the appearance of a shiny new part. Just don't look too closely, as wrinkles in the foil, surface imperfections, and seams make for a less than perfect finish.

If the trim piece is aluminum, it may be just a matter of polishing the part with a buffing wheel to remove the oxidation and bring back the shine; however, if the part is plated and hard to find, you may have no choice except to have the part replated.

Although there are many types of plating, the trim found on most pedal cars was usually either nickel or chromium plated. In order to replate any original parts, the old plating must first be removed. This involves placing the part in a chemical solution and stripping off the layers of plating by reverse electrolysis. Chrome plating is removed in one tank and nickel plating in another. After the old plating has been removed, the part is placed in an acid tank for derusting. The parts can now be inspected for any stress cracks or other damage. If a repair such as a weld is required, it must be done at this time.

Next, the parts are buffed to a mirror finish using various cutting compounds and buffing wheels. When buffing is completed, the parts are cleaned with a detergent solution to remove any residue from the buffing compound. Now the parts are given another reverse electrolysis bath, a rinse, and another dip in the acid tank to remove any fingerprints or traces of detergent. Only after a final rinse are the parts ready for the first layer of plating.

For the first layer, the parts are placed in a tank to be copper plated. Copper plating is necessary as it provides a good base for the next layer of plating, which is nickel. Also, a part that is mildly pitted can be copper plated, buffed, and replated several times if necessary to fill in the pits. This part of the process is critical in restorative plating and is usually required to replate badly deteriorated die cast parts. Depending on the situation, the parts can require anywhere from a half hour to four hours in the copper plating tank.

After rinsing, the parts are immersed in a nickel tank for approximately twenty minutes. A layer of nickel is deposited on the underlying copper coat. Rinsing is required once again before the parts are placed in the chrome tank. Once the parts are in the chrome tank it only takes a few minutes for an adequate layer to be deposited. As the parts are removed from the chrome tank they appear to be covered with a shiny golden film. The parts are then given a final rinse that removes this film and exposes a beautiful chrome finish.

TIPS TO REMEMBER REGARDING CHROME PLATING

- The quality of workmanship varies greatly among plating shops.

- Obtain a personal referral or ask to see a sample of the plating shop's work.

- Always discuss the work to be done with the plater to avoid disappointments.

- Not all plating shops want small jobs. Seek out a plater willing to handle your specific project.

- Consider using reproduction or N.O.S. parts if available, instead of trying to replate severely deteriorated parts.

- Nothing less than a mirror smooth surface produced by careful buffing is required for a bright plated finish.

- Send out the parts to be plated early in the project, as it usually takes several weeks for the plater to complete the job. Try to obtain a completion date for the plating.

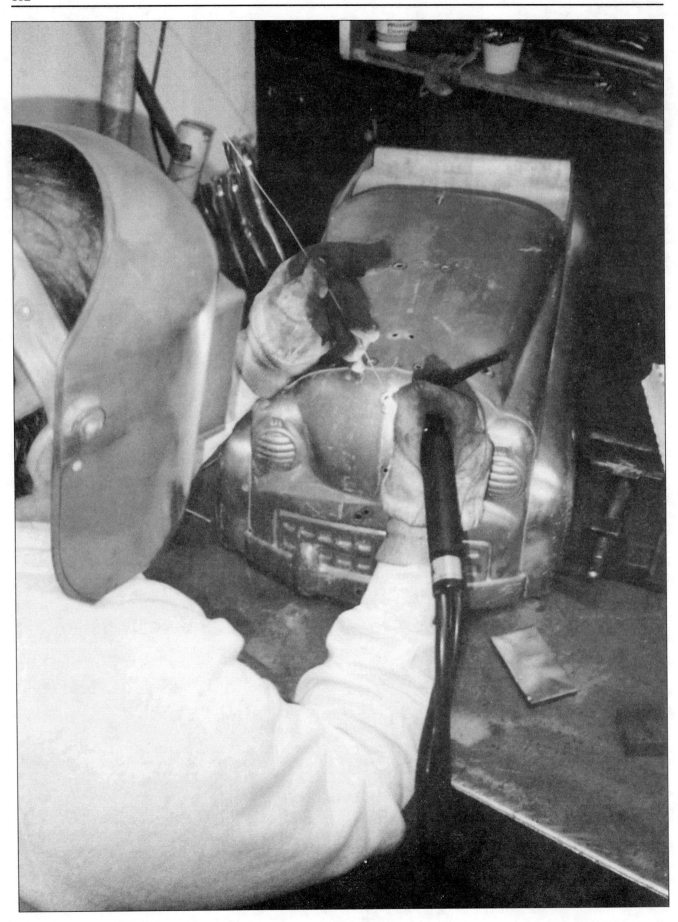

Chapter 9

Bodywork and Metal Repair

Once all the old paint and rust have been removed from the pedal car body, it is time to repair any damage that may have occurred to the metal. Damage may include dents, nonoriginal holes in the body, stress cracks, and deep scratches.

First consider tackling the dents, as they can be removed or at least minimized fairly easily. Pass your fingers over

All nonoriginal holes and any dents in the body are marked with a grease pencil for reference

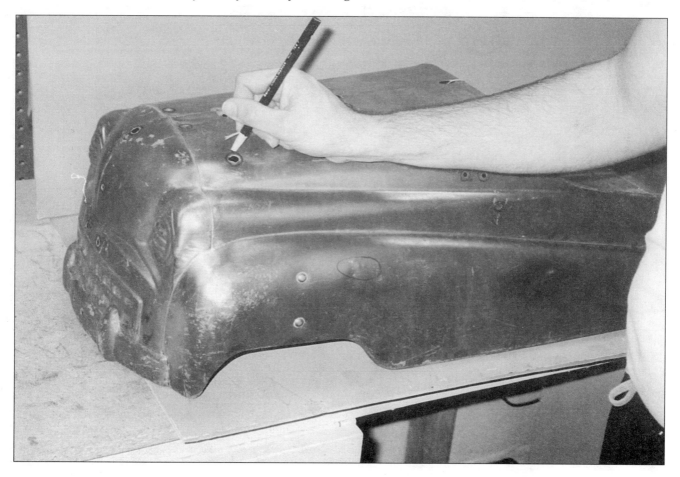

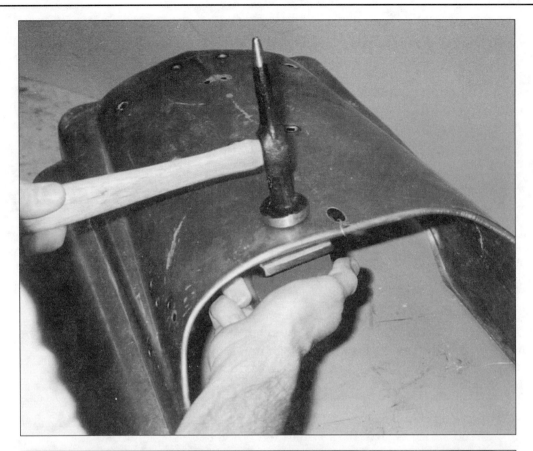

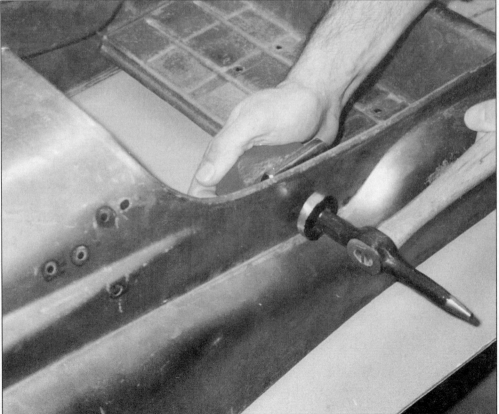

With the dolly on the opposite side of the dent to provide support, strike the flat face of the body hammer against the metal

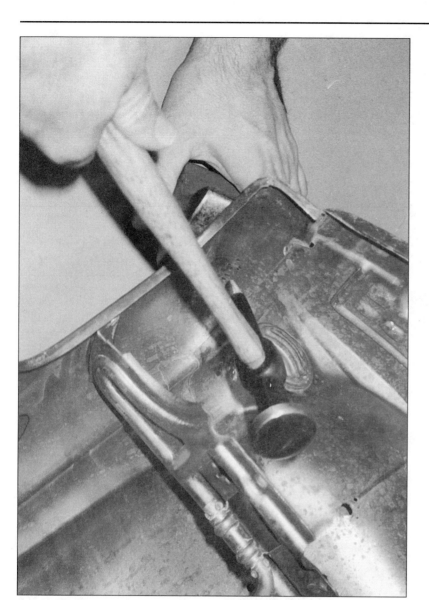

For a deep dent, strike the area with the pointed end of the body hammer

the entire surface of the pedal car to feel for any dents. If you discover any dents or nonoriginal holes, mark the area with a grease pencil. Next, using a body hammer and a dolly, bump out any accessible dents with the flat face of the hammer. For a deep or hard-to-reach dent use the pointed end of the body hammer to push out the metal. A ball peen hammer can be effective for dent removal on a curved inside surface. Most dents won't disappear 100 percent for the average restorer and that's to be expected; however, most dents can be smoothed out to within a few hundredths of an inch. When dents are minimized in this manner it is acceptable to add a slight amount of spot putty to smooth out the surface. Be patient and work the dent until it is flat. This way you can avoid using plastic body fillers. When the dents are removed, be sure to straighten out any damaged edges with a pair of pliers.

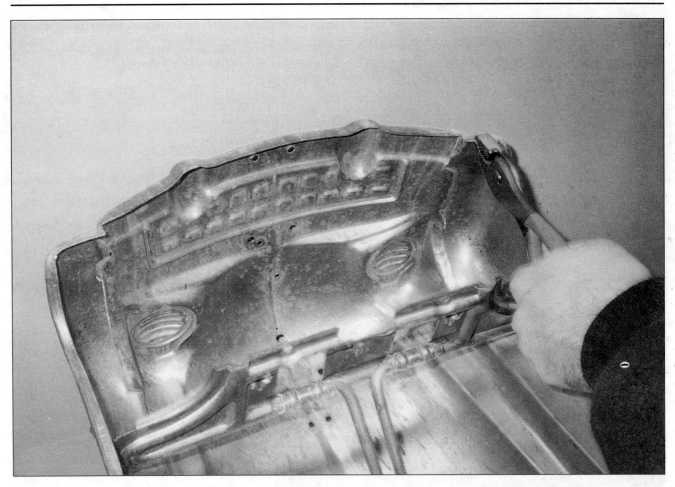

Pliers are used to straighten bent metal along the edges

The project Champion had several nonoriginal holes in the body and several dents along the sides. Each area that required attention was marked with a grease pencil for reference. Using a body hammer and a small universal dolly, the dents were bumped out one at a time. Several firm blows with the hammer were required to flatten out most of the dents. Along the bottom of the pedal car there were several places where the edge was bent. Using a pair of pliers, these areas were straightened.

Holes or stress cracks are best repaired by welding. In order to select the proper welding technique to fill in holes or repair stress cracks, one must remember that pedal car bodies are easily damaged by excess heat. The use of an oxyacetylene torch is not recommended because it will generate too much heat and can distort or further damage the pedal car. This method can also cause a buildup of oxides, which tends to contaminate the weld. Instead, bring the pedal car to someone who specializes in TIG (Tungsten Inert Gas) welding. TIG welding is an improved method of arc welding and uses electrical current and an inert gas such as helium or argon to produce a very clean, strong weld. With this type of welding, repairs can be made on metal-bodied pedal cars with a minimum of oxidation and distortion. This method works very well for filling holes in the body or repairing stress cracks. With the proper supervision and a little practice, it is not that difficult for a beginner to learn how to TIG weld. Unfortunately, the cost of equipment may be above the means of the average restorer. Not to worry, since TIG welding is widely used in industry and welding shops throughout the country. If you decide to repair a pedal car by this method, remember not to look directly at the arc, as eye damage can occur. It is standard practice for professional welders to wear a face shield and heavy gloves to protect themselves from molten metal.

After any dents and holes have been repaired, it is time to fill in surface irregularities with spot putty. Spot putty can be applied to clean bare metal or a primered surface. If a plastic body filler is to be used, it should be applied to "scuffed" bare metal only. When applying spot putty, use a putty knife or plastic spreader to place an even coat over the surface. Spot putty can be used to help smooth out dents, grinding marks, deep scratches, and pits in the pedal car's body. As a general rule, try not to build up spot putty over one-sixteenth of an inch thick. This will assure a suitable surface to apply primer and paint.

BODYWORK AND METAL REPAIR

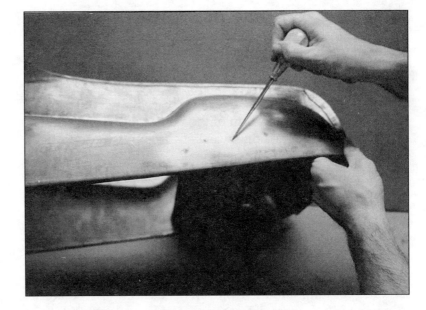

Check all spot welds to make sure they are still intact

Check for stress cracks around the mounting holes for the rear axle assembly

The pedal car was brought to Fairlane Welding in Dearborn, Michigan, to fill in several nonoriginal holes. First, the proper welding rod is selected by Master Welder Joe Lipani.

The TIG welder is switched on and the amperage is adjusted to match the thickness of the metal

With the machine properly grounded to the steel work top, it can be operated using a foot pedal

BODYWORK AND METAL REPAIR

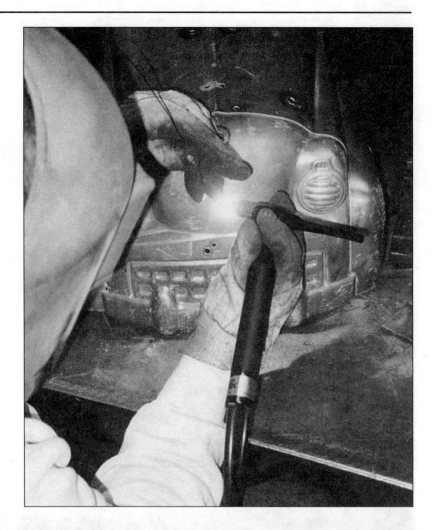

Here's where the skill comes into play: while holding the welding rod in one hand and striking an arc with the electrode in the other hand, the hole can be gradually filled

The first of many holes that needed repair. At a later time the weld can be ground smooth for an invisible repair.

No more Swiss cheese: all the holes in the rear bumper are filled

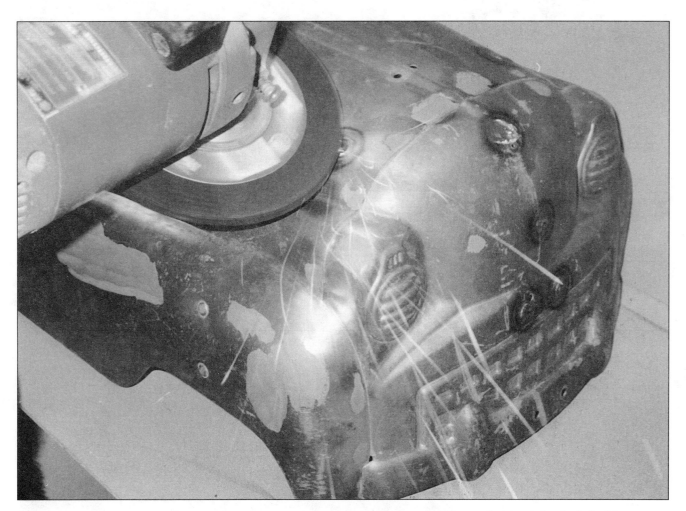

Using an electric grinder, the bulk of the excess weld is ground away

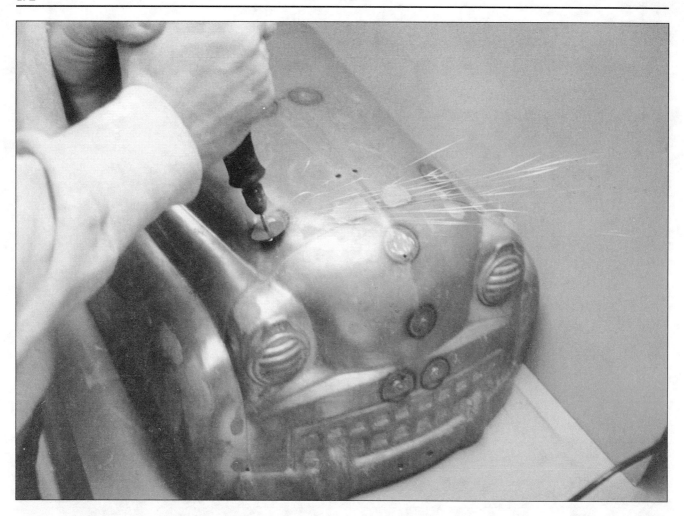

A rotary tool with a cut-off wheel is used to do the final blending of the repaired surface

Using a putty knife, slight irregularities in the body can be filled in with spot putty

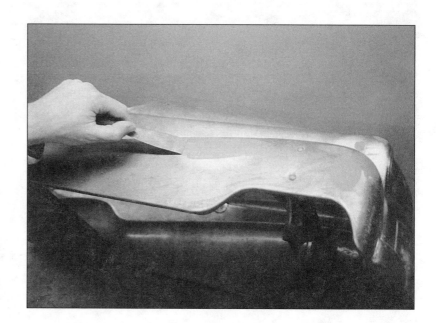

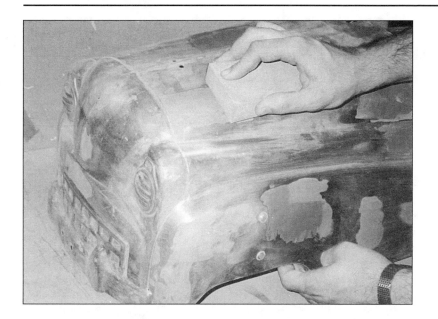

After the spot putty has dried for a few hours, it can be sanded using #220 grit wet/dry sandpaper. A foam sanding block works best on contoured areas.

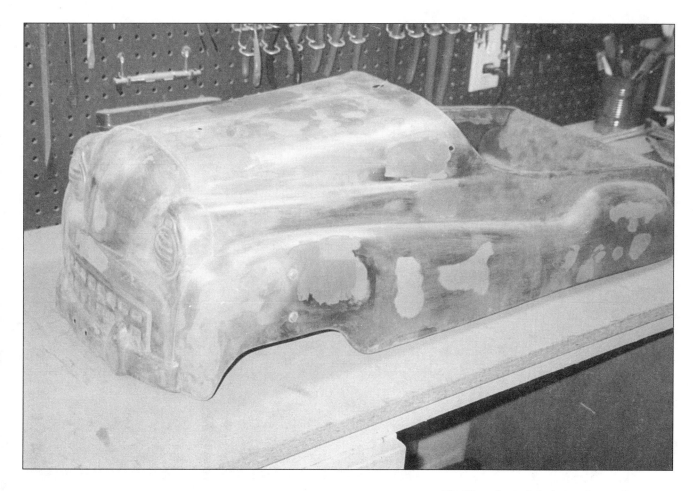

The Champion body had several areas that required spot putty, but most areas were less than 1/32-inch thick. Plastic body fillers were not used.

BODYWORK AND METAL REPAIR

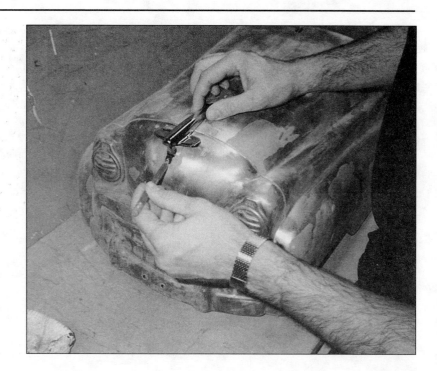

The front mounting hole is marked for the hood ornament. The original hole was damaged and had to be filled in.

Using a hand drill, a tiny hole is drilled into the hood to accept a screw for the hood ornament

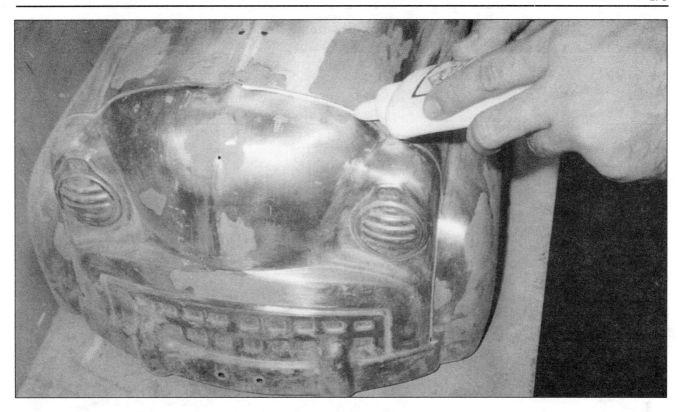

The hood is sealed to prevent paint from being absorbed unevenly into the seam

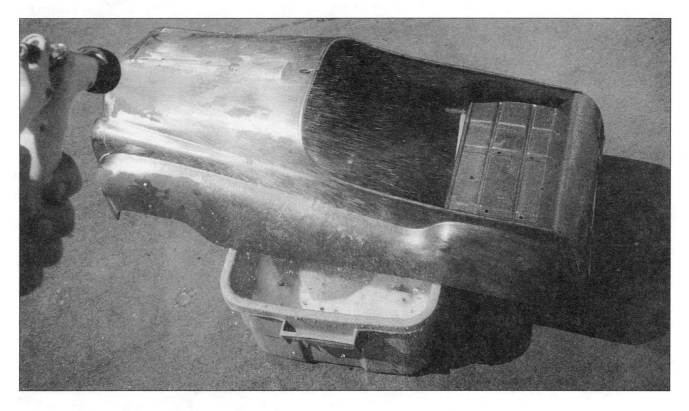

After being washed with a liquid detergent, the Champion body is rinsed and allowed to dry

BODYWORK AND METAL REPAIR

The Champion pedal car had several dents and repaired holes, in addition to a few scrapes along the sides, that needed to be filled with spot putty. (For a show car, you may want to consider lightly filling any exposed spot welds.) Using a putty knife, thin layers of spot putty were applied and allowed to dry for several hours. Be prepared to apply several thin coats rather than one thick coat. After the putty has hardened, use a sanding block and #220 grit wet/dry sandpaper to smooth out the repair. On a curved surface use a foam sanding block that will conform to the shape of the body. Go over the entire body with #220 grit followed by #320 grit sandpaper.

Now is a good time to test fit all the trim, including the windshield and the hood ornament. In some cases the surface of the body may require a slight adjustment to accom-

The Champion parts are scrubbed thoroughly and then rinsed. Compressed air may be used to speed the drying time.

modate the trim piece. For example, on the Champion a new hole had to be drilled for the hood ornament. The original hole was knocked off-center by a dent and had to be filled with weld. It is much easier to make adjustments now rather than trying to work on the body after it is painted.

Most pedal cars have seams, some of which can absorb paint into them. In some cases this results in gaps along the seam. To guard from this happening, a small amount of seam sealer or paintable caulk should be smoothed into the seams. This absolutely does not mean to completely fill in the seam; rather, the seam is filled and most of the caulk is wiped away. The caulk that remains protects any paint from being absorbed into the seam. When the seam sealer has thoroughly dried, the pedal car body and all associated parts can be cleaned with a degreasing detergent and then rinsed. This will remove all the dust and grit that has accumulated on the pedal car. The pedal car should be dried in the sunshine, or compressed air may be used to speed the drying process. With the pedal car clean and dry, it is now ready for the next step in the restoration process—the application of primer and paint.

Top to bottom: supplies necessary for paint application; the new finish on the project Champion is as smooth as glass and has a deep shine

CHAPTER 10

PAINT APPLICATION

Of all the steps that are involved in a pedal car restoration, the most intimidating process may be applying the finish. The measuring, mixing, and spraying of automotive finishes can be confusing to the uninitiated. Typically, the novice painter will have a few problems and even an expert restorer can encounter difficulties.

Almost everyone has heard a story in which a painting disaster has occurred. Not long ago a restorer had just completed spraying a beautiful enamel finish on his pedal car. Since the garage needed a little ventilation, the restorer decided to open the overhead door. In came the fresh air, along with a blizzard of fuzz from the seeds of a nearby cottonwood tree. Needless to say, the fuzz landed on the freshly painted pedal car and completely ruined the paint job. Does this story sound a bit intimidating? Certainly. Can only commercial body shops produce quality paint jobs? Hardly.

There is a good reason why a restorer should pay close attention to the way a pedal car is painted. No matter how expertly the rest of the restoration was completed, people tend to judge a car based on its paint job. If a pedal car gleams with a brilliant finish, everyone wants to know "who did the paint." Today, an ever increasing number of restorers working out of their home workshops can proudly say "I did."

When approaching the task of painting a pedal car or when contracting out to a professional, you should have a basic knowledge of automotive paints and application methods. This chapter does not pretend to be an introductory text on automotive painting. Rather, it will show some of the basic techniques and helpful hints that can be employed when painting a pedal car in the home garage. In this manner, you

PAINT APPLICATION

A trip to the automotive paint store can be a bit overwhelming. Sound advice from a helpful technician is a good way to start a painting project.

may avoid some of the more common mistakes usually made by beginners.

BASIC FORMS OF AUTOMOTIVE PAINTS

Lacquers

Lacquer paint is a good choice for the beginner because it is fast-drying. After a color is selected it is mixed with a recommended amount of lacquer thinner. Normally lacquer paint is thinned 100-150 percent for use in a spray gun. When sprayed, lacquer dries very quickly, which lessens the chance for runs or dust to interfere with the finish. Since lacquer dries fast, the painter is able to recoat the project al-

Right: Lacquer thinner is typically sold in one gallon cans

Far right: Reducer is available for different temperature ranges. This particular product has a workable temperature range of 50-70°F.

most immediately, or if a flaw in the paint needs to be corrected it can be done that same day.

On the negative side, lacquer paint is not known for its durability and it has a few other drawbacks as well. When lacquer is first applied it has a high gloss, but as the paint dries it becomes considerably duller. To obtain a high level of gloss, the paint must be rubbed out using a buffing wheel and rubbing compounds. Hand rubbing can also be done, but this is time consuming. Be aware that since lacquer paint is sprayed on in thin layers it can be easily damaged by improper power-buffing techniques.

If a restorer chooses to paint a pedal car with lacquer, the results can be spectacular. After building up several layers of paint, rubbing compounds can be used to develop a mirror finish; however, creating a nice shine on the underside of the pedal car can be difficult and time consuming. When restoring a pedal car that will be used again by a child, lacquer would not be the best choice.

A catalyst can be added to acrylic enamel for increased durability

Acrylic Enamels

Generally known for their durability, acrylic enamels cure to a hard glossy finish and are used extensively by the automotive industry. Acrylic enamel is mixed with a reducer in order to be sprayed. The amount of reducer added can vary anywhere from 35 to 50 percent. One of the big advantages of acrylic enamel is its hiding power. One coat of acrylic enamel is thicker than several coats of lacquer. Enamels do not require rubbing out to achieve a high gloss.

Enamels do have some drawbacks. The longer drying period means airborne contaminants have a greater chance of settling on the finish, and a run or other problem usually can't be corrected the same day since the paint will still be soft. Another small disadvantage is noticed when painting with more than one color or when masking off an area. When removing masking tape along an area that has been painted with enamel, a ridge will usually form due to the thickness of the paint.

If you choose to use an enamel to paint your pedal car, a clean spray area is a must. You may want to rent a spray booth for a day or create a temporary one using plastic dropcloths in the home garage. A nice enamel paint job on a pedal car will have a deep shine and will be durable enough to handle a few bumps and scuffs without showing any damage. Don't worry if the finish coat doesn't end up being 100 percent dust free. Enamel can be color sanded and rubbed out to remove these flaws.

Generally lacquers and enamels don't mix; however, this type of high build primer surfacer is thinned with lacquer and is designed to be used under enamels or urethanes

Urethanes

Considered by some restorers as the "Cadillac of paints," polyurethane enamels or urethane paints are gaining in popularity. Known for their high gloss and "slick feel," urethanes are also resistant to abrasion and harsh fuels. Essentially, urethanes are a two-part system requiring the addition of a catalytic hardening agent. When the catalyst is added the finish hardens very quickly into an incredibly durable surface. You may already be familiar with the properties of similar components that are found in two-part epoxy.

Urethane is an excellent choice for pedal cars. Unfortunately it is very expensive compared to other types of paints and has similar drawbacks to regular enamels. If color sanding is to be done it can be difficult and should be done the day after the paint is applied. For a show car in particular you may want to consider using urethane for the ultimate finish.

Metallic Finishes

There are several types of custom finishes in which metal or metal-like flakes are added to cause the paint to sparkle. Pearl paints consist of an iridescent color that is usually sprayed over a special base coat of white or black. The effect is similar to the shimmering surface of a pearl or the inside of an oyster shell. Candy colors are vivid, translucent paints that are sprayed over a gold or silver metallic base coat. A candy color will allow light to pass through it and reflect off of the metallic base coat, resulting in a deep, brilliant color considered by many to be far more exciting than ordinary solid color paints.

Metallic finishes look nice and are a favorite choice for many restorers who are working on custom pedal cars. Custom projects aren't the only candidates for metallics, however, as some pedal cars were originally painted with these finishes from the factory. The restorer should be aware that metal flake, pearl, and candy finishes do require more care to apply and some require a clear top coat for protection. The beginner may want to seek some assistance before spraying a metallic finish.

Primers

No matter what type of paint is selected, it needs a special base to adhere properly. This special base is called primer, which is actually just a flat paint with good adhesion properties. Some types of primers have extra additives that help to fill in scratches or other surface defects and are called primer surfacers. Also available are primer sealers, which enable the restorer to spray one type of paint over another type.

Spraying primer is easier than applying the finish coat of paint since the level of gloss is not a factor. You must always remember to use a compatible type of primer with the selected paint.

Paint Additives

Retarders are useful additives that slow the drying time of enamels and lacquers in hot weather. These products help flow out the paint and prevent it from drying too quickly and dulling the finish.

A few drops of fisheye eliminator can help assure a uniform finish

Fisheye eliminator is another product that can help a restorer avoid problems. Fisheyes are round shiny spots that can appear in the top coat. These spots are caused by microscopic trace elements of silicone that can sometimes hide in tiny surface imperfections. Both retarder and fisheye eliminator should be added directly to the strained paint.

Metal-prep is a chemical etch solution that prepares a bare steel surface for painting. Alumi-prep is a similar solution that is used on bare aluminum. If you choose to have a pedal car commercially stripped to bare metal, it is not necessary to use any type of etching solution.

Grease and wax remover is used to remove body oils, dirt, wax, and silicones from a surface prior to painting. This product should be used prior to priming a pedal car and prior to applying the paint. Some restorers like to wear gloves to prevent body oils from being deposited on bare metal or primed parts.

When using any of these additives it is critical to read and follow the manufacturer's directions included on the product.

After cleaning a surface with grease and wax remover, the residue must be allowed to evaporate completely before applying a coat of primer or paint. If the grease and wax remover is not allowed to dry completely, a reaction could take place that would cause the finish to "check," or wrinkle.

A wise painter wears the proper gear, including a respirator, goggles, and coveralls

PAINT APPLICATION

Paper mixing cups, filter funnels, and mixing sticks are basic supplies for painting a pedal car

MISCELLANEOUS SUPPLIES

There are a few other items that are required for a painting project. Don't start without a good respirator to filter out harmful vapors. Goggles to protect the eyes and coveralls for the body is standard practice.

Naturally, a spray gun and air compressor would be preferred over using a paint brush. Don't laugh—early automotive painters applied layer upon layer of black lacquer with a brush and painstakingly rubbed it out to a mirror finish.

You should have on hand several mixing cups, filter funnels, and mixing sticks. Some painters like to use a scotch brite pad between coats of primer or paint. If a paint job needs to be color sanded, 1000 and 2000 grit wet/dry sandpaper and a special rubber sanding block should be purchased. For removing dust and lint prior to painting, a tack cloth is needed.

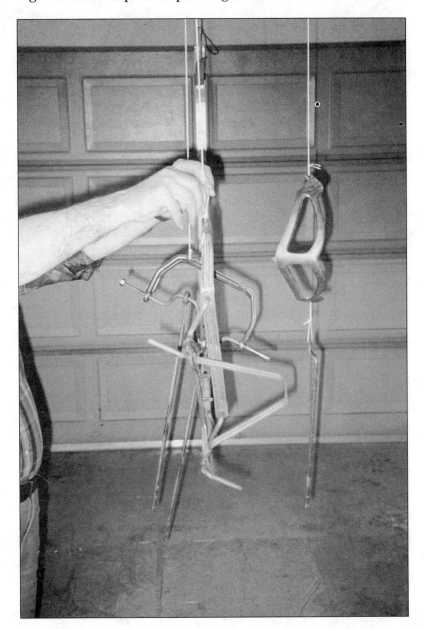

Whoever said there are no strings attached to painting a pedal car? Some of the Champion's parts are being hung from strings to facilitate painting.

PREPARING FOR PAINTING

It would be nice if everyone had access to a downdraft spray painting booth like the ones used in some professional body shops. The reality is that many restorers will paint a pedal car in their own garage or shed. With a little care, the garage can be turned into a suitable place to apply a sprayed-on finish.

First clear the garage of any vehicles and extraneous clutter, then sweep and wash the floor to remove most of the dirt and dust. When the floor has dried, spread a dropcloth to protect the work area from overspray. Some restorers like to use disposable plastic drop cloths to cover the floor and walls of their garage. Don't forget to wipe down the airhose between the spray gun and compressor to remove any contaminants. It is a good idea to have a water/oil separator on the air line to remove any impurities that may be present in the compressed air.

In the case of the project Champion it was beneficial to hang the undercarriage parts, steering rod, and windshield in order to reach all sides with the spray gun. The rims, steering wheel, and body were placed on clean milk crates, as they would be sprayed one side at a time. The crates also served to raise the

The rims and steering wheel are placed horizontally for painting. This position seems to discourage runs from occurring.

After spraying the underside, the front of the rims and steering wheel are primed

The Champion's body receives a coat of primer

After spraying, the primer coat should be lightly sanded with fine sandpaper or gone over with a 3M pad

parts off the ground away from possible contamination. All the parts were then wiped down with grease and wax remover and allowed to dry. As a final step before spraying the primer, a tack cloth was used to remove any dust or lint.

PRIMER APPLICATION

The first step in the application of the primer is to mix the primer or surfacer per the manufacturer's directions and set the compressor to the recommended pressure for your spray gun. For the Champion, a lacquer-based, high build primer surfacer was used. The primer was thinned 150 percent with lacquer thinner and the air compressor's regulator was set at 35 PSI. The underside of the body, the rims, and the steering wheel were sprayed first. When they were dry to the touch the parts were turned over in order to spray the opposite side. While waiting for the underside of the body to dry, the hanging parts were primed. To assure an adequate base, four coats of primer surfacer were applied to all areas. The parts were left

PAINT APPLICATION

To prepare for paint, the wheels are wiped down with grease and wax remover. When dry, a tack cloth is used to remove any contaminants.

Don't forget to degrease and tack the body, including the underside

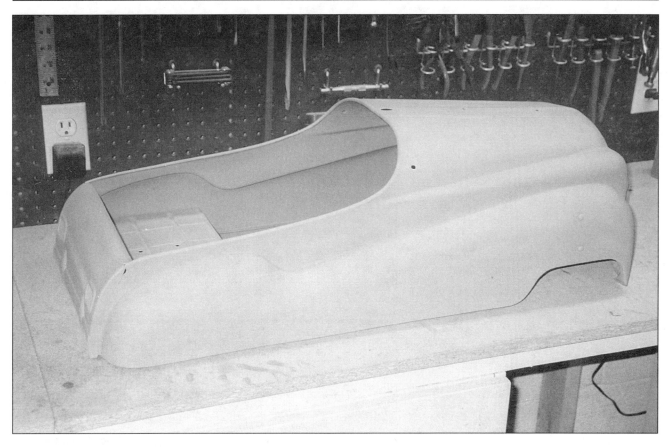

The Champion body in primer

to dry overnight although the primer surfacer could be sanded in less than one hour after being applied.

The next day the undercarriage parts were taken down and gone over with a 3M pad. When this step was completed the parts were hung, degreased, and tacked off. At this time the wheels were lightly scuffed and thoroughly cleaned. Attention could now be directed to the pedal car body. Both the underside and exterior of the body were sanded with #400 grit wet/dry sandpaper and both sides were degreased and gone over with a tack cloth.

PAINT APPLICATION

With the parts and body ready to accept a finish, the paint was opened and gently mixed with a wooden paint stick. The blue acrylic enamel was poured into a mixing cup and reduced by approximately 40 to 50 percent per the manufacturer's directions. To this mixture a few drops of "Smoothie" was added, along with a small amount of "Wet Look" catalyst. The paint was then poured into the spray gun's reservoir through a paper filter funnel. Now that the spray gun was filled, the air hose was connected and the pressure was adjusted on the compressor's regulator. For this particular application, the regulator was set at 45 PSI.

Blue acrylic enamel is poured into a mixing cup. Before pouring any paint from the can it should be gently stirred.

PAINT APPLICATION

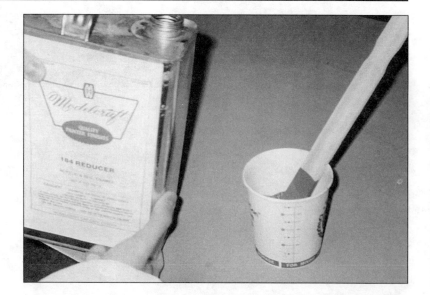

Reducer is added to the enamel. Up to 50 percent reduction is acceptable.

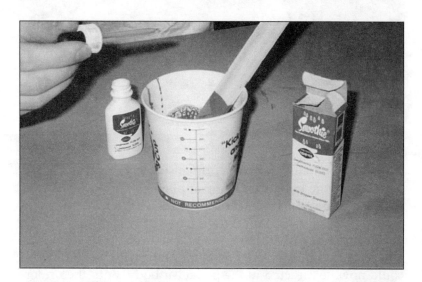

A few drops of "Smoothie" are added to help flow out the paint and eliminate fisheyes

A small amount of "Wet Look" catalyst is added. This product improves durability and allows recoating at any time.

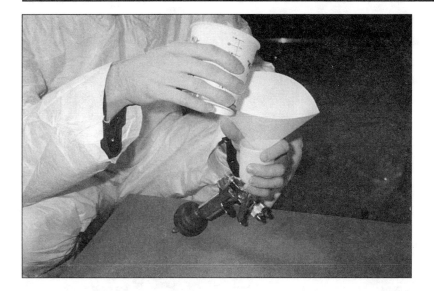

Using a paper filter funnel, the paint mixture is poured into the spray gun's reservoir

The spray gun is attached to the air supply line from the compressor. Note the in-line filter on the spray gun to remove contaminants.

The regulator on the air compressor is dialed to the proper pressure

PAINT APPLICATION

Always test the spray pattern on a piece of scrap material. Adjust the spray gun to produce a uniform band of coverage.

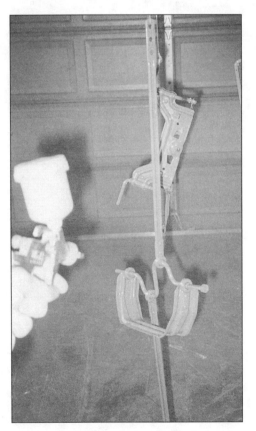

Blue acrylic enamel is sprayed on the hanging parts

Before any paint was sprayed on the project, a test pattern was shot from the spray gun on a scrap piece of cardboard. The ideal pattern will deposit a uniform band of paint across the surface. If the pattern is too streamlike, a run can easily occur; if the pattern is too wide, the surface can end up looking like an orange peel. Always try to keep the nozzle of the spray gun parallel to the surface. Don't stop painting a section once you have started. The idea when painting enamel is to keep the surrounding area glossy and blend it with the leading edge of paint that is emitted from the nozzle. All hanging parts were given three coats of paint and would take on a final finish that would require no additional work.

Before the final coat is sprayed on the body, it is a good idea to paint the rims, steering wheel, and windshield. In fact, these parts could be painted first if you prefer. On the Champion, three coats of white were applied to these parts with no additional work being required for an acceptable finish.

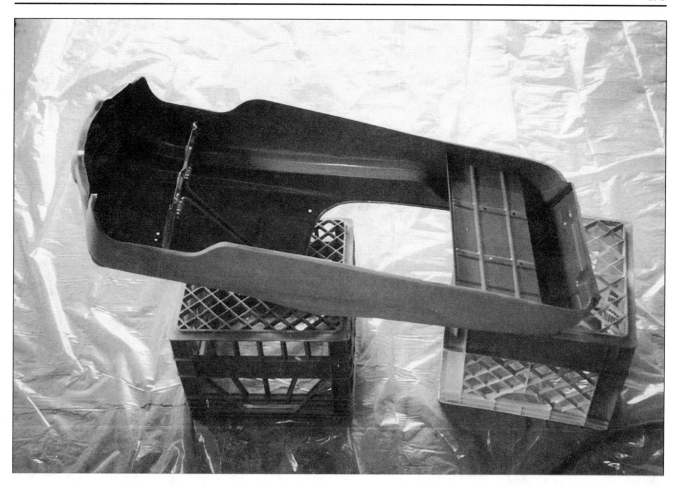

Start painting the body by spraying the underside. When dry to the touch, turn the car over and spray the exterior.

The rims, steering wheel, and windshield of the Champion are painted white. Painting these parts one side at a time while they are lying horizontally discourages runs from forming.

194

In order to paint the center of the wheel in blue, liquid mask is brushed along the edges of the wheel

PAINTING WHEELS IN TWO COLORS

Many restorers like to apply a two-tone finish on the wheels, and such was the case with the Champion. It was decided to mask off the edges of the wheel and to paint the center of the wheel the same blue color as the body. The best way to handle masking off a circle or an irregular shape is to use a liquid mask product.

A liquid mask is a water soluble solution that brushes on wet and dries to form a flexible "rubbery" coating. This coating can be trimmed with a sharp knife in any shape or configuration that the restorer requires. Liquid mask was brushed all around the edges of the Champion's wheels. When dry, the mask was trimmed and the excess material was peeled away. To prevent contamination from overspray, the back side of the wheels were masked off with plastic wrap secured by painter's masking tape.

After tacking off the center of the rims, they were sprayed with the same blue enamel that will be used on the body. The next day the remaining mask was removed to reveal a nice clean line between the white edge of the wheel and the blue center.

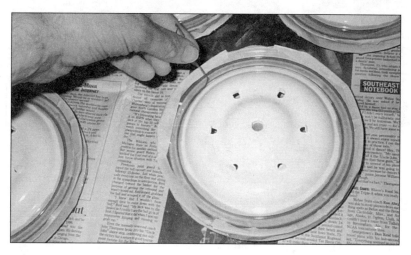

When the mask dries it can be trimmed with a sharp knife and peeled away

The wheels are now sprayed with blue enamel

After the blue paint has dried for twenty-four hours the mask can be peeled away. The result is a crisp edge between painted areas.

FINAL PAINT APPLICATION

Attention was now directed toward preparation for the final coats of paint on the pedal car body. Initially the body was given two coats of enamel while on the milk crates. These first two layers helped level out the surface by filling in tiny imperfections and allowing the underside to receive adequate coverage. The second two layers were applied a few days later while the pedal car was in a hanging position. Applying the paint in two stages minimized the likelihood of runs forming due to several heavy layers of paint.

Before the final two coats of enamel were applied, the pedal car body was wet sanded with #600 grit wet/dry sandpaper. A rubber sanding block worked well and conformed to the rounded contour of the Champion's body. When all areas had received attention, the body was once again degreased and tacked off. Next the pedal car was suspended from the ceiling with nylon string. After another mixture of paint was prepared and loaded into the spray gun, the final two coats of enamel were applied to the pedal car. After allowing several days for the paint to cure, the car will be ready to reassemble.

For most restorers the finish would be adequate at this stage; however, some restorers might experience problems such as runs, orange peel, or dust that needs to be eliminated from the final finish. One method of solving these problems is to color sand the paint. Color sanding involves going over the finish with ultra fine sandpaper in the 1000-2000 grit range to produce a level finish. Sanding is accomplished using plenty of water and a special rubber sanding block.

Since color sanding will dull the finish, rubbing compounds must be used to bring back the shine. A power buffer can be used on the large areas, but hand rubbing will be necessary in those hard-to-reach places. The novice should seek advice from the local automotive paint store and practice power buffing techniques on a test project.

In many cases, certain parts of a pedal car's body were painted to highlight its details. For instance, on the Champion the bumpers, headlights, and taillights were painted silver. The best way to mask around these areas is to use a liquid mask product. To begin, paint the liquid mask around the lights and bumpers.

Returning to the body after a few days, it can be lightly water sanded with #600 wet/dry sandpaper.

PAINT APPLICATION

When dry, cut around the outline of these areas and peel away the unwanted section of mask. Next, using newspaper and painter's masking tape, cover any exposed areas of the pedal car to protect from overspray. Clean the area with a tack rag and spray a thin layer of primer sealer. Once the primer sealer has dried, scuff lightly, tack off, and spray with silver paint. When the remaining mask is removed, the silver accents will complete the original paint scheme of the Champion.

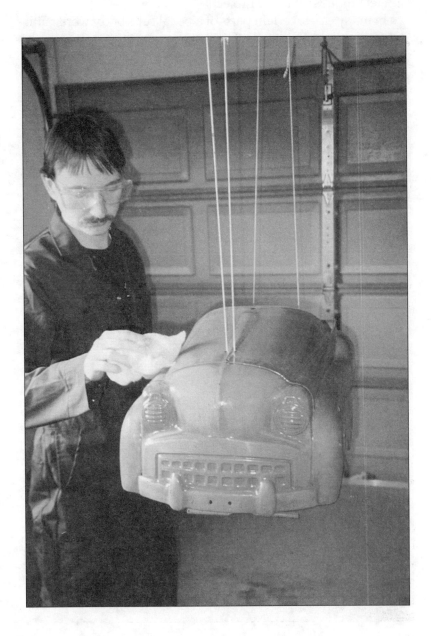

The Champion body is hung by nylon string in order to paint the underside and the exterior at one time. The body should be wiped down with grease and wax remover and a tack cloth.

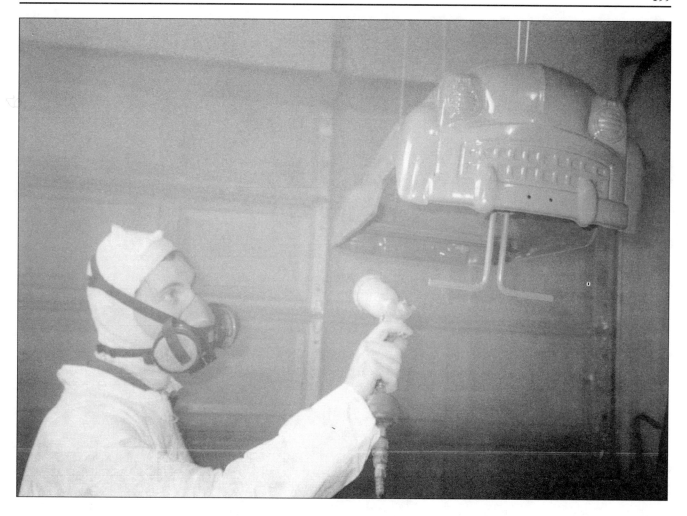

Crouching low to access the underside of the pedal car, painter Mel Davis applies the finishing coats of enamel

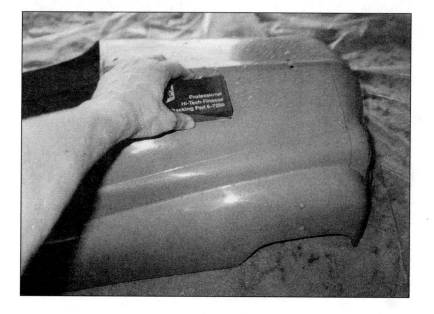

After drying for a few days, the exterior of the pedal car can be color sanded with #1000 and #2000 grit wet/dry sandpaper and a rubber sanding block

PAINT APPLICATION

Since color sanding leaves fine scratches, the exterior finish should be rubbed out with coarse and fine buffing compound. Be extremely careful when using a power buffer so as not to "burn through" the finish.

Liquid mask is painted around the headlights and the front grille

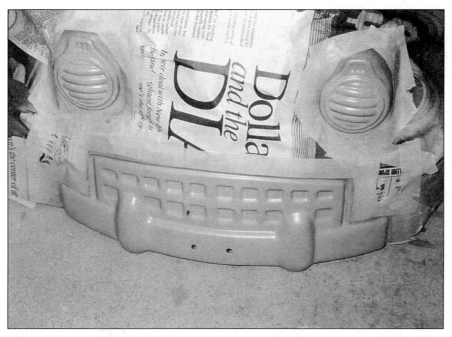

After the liquid mask has dried, it is trimmed and an additional mask is made using newspaper and painter's masking tape. A light coat of primer sealer is applied to help the next layer of paint adhere.

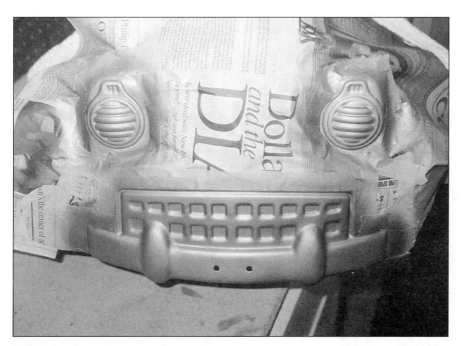

Two light coats of silver enamel are applied to the headlights and front grille of the Champion

*When the mask is removed, the front end has been
returned to factory-new condition*

*The rear bumper and taillights need to
be masked also*

PAINT APPLICATION

A light coat of primer sealer is applied, followed by two coats of silver enamel

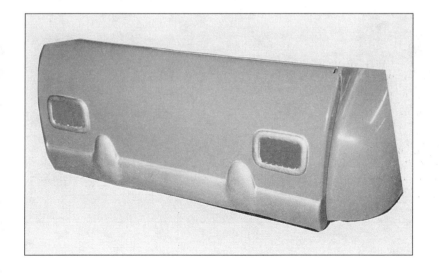

With the mask removed, the rear bumper and taillights highlight the rear end nicely. Though not original, some restorers like to paint the lenses of the taillight bright red.

The tire and wheel of the Champion before and after restoration

CHAPTER 11

TIRES AND UPHOLSTERY

Early pedal cars had large, spoked metal wheels with 3/8-inch or 1/2-inch rubber tires. During the early 1900s it became popular to use an extruded rubber tire secured to the rim by a wire. A length of extruded rubber was trimmed slightly longer than the circumference of the rim and a wire was inserted through the center of the rubber. The wire and rubber were then placed around the rim and were mounted in a special tire machine that spread the rubber apart slightly so the two ends of the wire could be hooked together and trimmed. When the rubber tire was released from the machine it would spring back together, thus hiding the wire. All that was visible was a seam between the two ends of the rubber. The wire held the tire securely to the rim even under hard use.

In 1923 the Cole 8 was the first full-size automobile to offer pneumatic or "balloon" tires. Balloon tires were filled with air and served to cushion the ride over a bumpy road. The design of balloon tires was soon adapted for wheel goods. By the mid-1930s several manufacturers offered balloon tires on their deluxe models of pedal cars. American National featured 10 x 2.50-inch Firestone pneumatic tires on its Skippy Airflow Chrysler and on several other models.

The next decade brought World War II, and the conservation of metal and rubber during the war caused a large decline in the use of balloon tires on pedal cars. During the postwar years pedal car manufacturers relied on the time-tested method of extruded rubber secured with a wire. On full-size cars, the tubeless tire was introduced in 1950.

By the 1960s, one-piece molded rubber tires came into popular use on pedal cars and pedal tractors. Molded tires were slightly smaller than the wheel and could be stretched onto the rim. This type of tire eliminated the extra step of adding a piece of wire and produced a seamless fit.

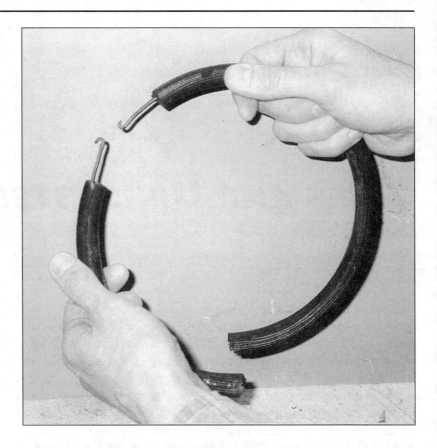

The wire tie method was popular for securing the tire to the wheel on pedal cars. A length of wire was passed through a piece of extruded rubber tire. The ends of the wire could be hooked or tied together to firmly attach the tire to the wheel.

Shown is the "Excelsior Tire Machine" used to secure rubber tires to the rims of wheel goods

The 1970s brought the rapid decline of the pedal car and an increase in the use of plastics. During this time period, some wheeled toys had one-piece rims and tires molded out of plastic. Today many modern versions of the pedal car have a plastic wheel/tire combination.

MAKING A ROLL-ON TIRE FOR A PEDAL CAR

Several pedal car parts companies offer pre-made roll-on tires for the restorer. These work perfectly well; however, some restorers may want to make their own tires, especially if their pedal car has an odd-size wheel. The process is relatively straightforward and starts with the purchase of several feet of extruded tire rubber from a pedal car parts supplier. If you are not sure of the size or diameter of the rubber, send a sample piece of the old tire to the supplier as a guide.

Once you have obtained the tire rubber, wrap a length of it around the wheel in order to take a measurement. Use a white grease pencil and mark the tire about three-fourths of an inch less than the circumference of the wheel. Next use a PVC tubing cutter, which is available at most home centers, to make an even cut across the rubber. If you use a utility knife or fine-toothed saw, you may experience some difficulty in slicing the rubber correctly.

After the rubber is cut to the proper length, apply a thin layer of Bondini cement or similar adhesive to one end of the rubber. Line up the grooves in the tire rubber and press the two ends together. Once the ends are together, don't try to readjust the fit, as this will tend to weaken the bond. Apply firm pressure on the seam for approximately one minute in order for the adhesive to set. After a minute, set the tire aside to cure for at least another fifteen minutes before being installed on the wheel. Stretch or roll on the tire from the back side of the wheel to prevent a rub mark or scuff from occurring to the exterior of the wheel. Repeat the process for each rim until all four wheels are fit with tires.

To begin making a roll-on tire for the Champion, bulk extruded rubber measuring 5/8-inch in diameter is placed around the rim in the tire groove

Using a white grease pencil, the tire rubber is marked for length approximately 3/4-inch shorter than the circumference of the rim

The tire rubber is cut to length using a PVC tubing cutter. This tool works far better than a utility knife or saw.

TIRES AND UPHOLSTERY

Place the length of rubber around the wheel for a preliminary fit. If the rubber is too long the tire will be loose; cutting it too short will make it difficult to stretch it onto the wheel.

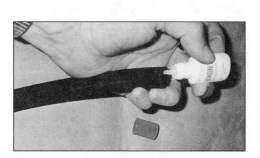

Apply a thin layer of Bondini adhesive to one side of the tire rubber

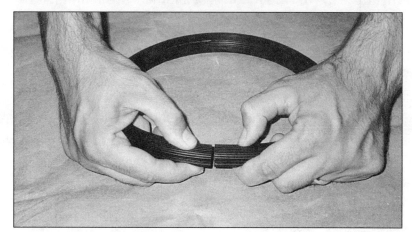

While being careful to line up the grooves in the tire, press the two ends of the tire together and hold in place for one minute

Allow the adhesive to cure for at least fifteen minutes and then "roll on" the tire around the wheel. Be sure to stretch the tire on from the back side of the rim.

PEDAL CAR UPHOLSTERY

Pedal cars traditionally do not have very much upholstery. Pedal car manufacturers realized their products would be exposed to the elements and therefore would be subject to deterioration. Moisture and the sun's rays degrade fabric at an accelerated rate, not to mention wear and tear from children.

Some early pedal cars had leather or horsehair upholstery, while others used velvet or naugahyde as a seat covering. By the 1920s many types of pedal cars had convertible tops made of heavy fabric and some models even had upholstered rumble seats. After the Second World War most pedal cars merely had a seat pad. As the years passed, seat pads with stitching were replaced with other materials. Textured pressed paper, vinyl, and then plastic were all used to make an inexpensive, single-layer seat cover.

Upholstery work requires a commercial sewing machine to penetrate heavy fabrics. You may want to purchase a ready-made seat pad or use the services of a professional automotive upholstery shop.

The pedal car has undergone an amazing transformation

CHAPTER 12

FINAL ASSEMBLY

Now that all parts have been reconditioned, it is time to re-assemble the pedal car. Begin by lubricating any moving parts with lithium grease. Add a dab to all bearings, linkage, and axles. Use a clean cloth to wipe away any excess grease.

Install the wheels on the rear axle and the front steering assembly. The drive wheel is secured with a nut, while the other three wheels require a washer and cotter pin. Install the hubcaps once the wheels are in place. When bending the tabs over the hubcaps, use a standard screwdriver with the end wrapped in masking tape. This will help prevent damage to the paint on the tabs. If the paint on the tabs happens to become chipped, touch up the area with a small paintbrush dipped in leftover paint.

Turn the pedal car body over and attach the axle hanger and rear wheels to the underside of the Champion with four truss head screws and square nuts. Be sure to place a pad or towel underneath the pedal car so as not to scratch the new paint. Insert the connecting straps onto the pedal rods. The holes in the connecting straps allow for some adjustment depending on the length of the rider's legs. Slide the new rubber pedals over the pedal rods and secure each pedal in place with a washer and cotter pin. If the pedal car is to be used by a child, bend the cotter pin so that it won't have any sharp, protruding edges that could cause an injury.

Next install the front steering assembly and wheels to the front end support. It is better to slip the front brace underneath the front bumper and then slide the assembly onto the front support. Secure the assembly with two truss head screws and square nuts through the front support. Use two additional screw/nut combinations to attach the front brace to the front bumper.

Slide the steering shaft through the steering assembly and insert the bent end into the steering link. Secure the shaft with a washer and cotter pin. The pedal car is now ready to turn

212

Mylar Application Instructions

A

Place the pedal car at a comfortable working level. Get masking tape, scissors and a squeegee for this job.
Note: Use a credit card or stiff I.D. card as a squeegee.

B

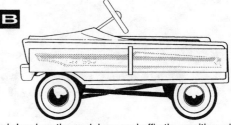

Level decal on the pedal car and affix the position with a piece of masking tape.

C

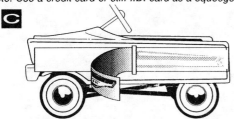

Starting from front of pedal car, peel the transfer tape away from the backing paper until you reach the masking tape.

D

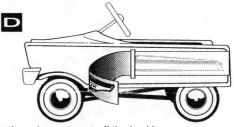

Use the scissors to cut off the backing paper.

E

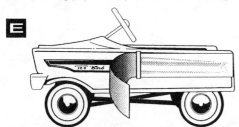

Use a squeegee to press the decal onto the car by holding the loose end of the decal slightly taunt & working from the strip of masking tape toward the front of the car.

F

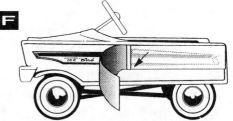

Carefully peel back the masking tape off of the car,

G

Trim the excess masking tape off as closely as possible to

H

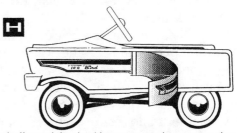

Peel off remaining backing paper and squeegee down the remainder of the decal working from center to the rear area.

I

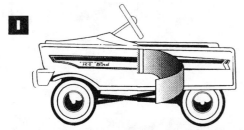

Completely remove the entire piece of transfer tape slowly.

J

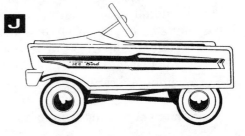

Typical application takes about 10 minutes each side.

PEDAL CAR GRAPHICS
1207 CHARTER OAK DRIVE
TAYLORS, SOUTH CAROLINA 29687

right side up in order to complete the final assembly. Install the windshield using two screws and acorn nuts, and attach the steering wheel with an acorn nut as well. The seat pad can now be installed. Place the seat pad in position and mark the mounting hole from underneath the seat. Punch a hole in the seat pad using a leather punch and secure the seat pad to the pedal car using a truss head screw backed with a square nut.

At last the airplane hood ornament can find its rightful place on the hood of the newly restored Champion. Slide the ornament's tabs in place on the top of the hood and secure the front of the ornament with a small machine screw.

The last step is to apply the graphics. Using a ruler and a grease pencil, mark the location of the graphics on the body. On the Champion the seat back label was applied first and then the side graphics. A small adjustment had to be made to move the letters in "Champion" closer together in order to match the original spacing. Follow the steps at left as outlined by Bob Ellsworth for the proper application of mylar graphics.

The pedal car is now complete and has undergone a thorough and meticulous restoration. At this point you will feel a great amount of satisfaction for a job well done. Now it's time to relax, grab a cold drink, and ... think about the next pedal car you want to restore!

Champion parts that are required for the final assembly

FINAL ASSEMBLY

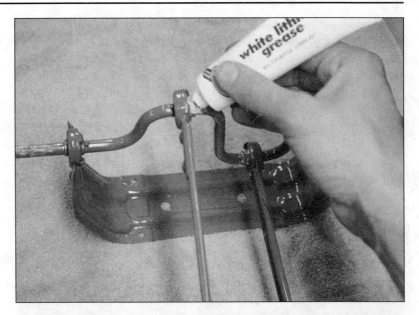

Using white lithium grease, lubricate all moving parts of the undercarriage

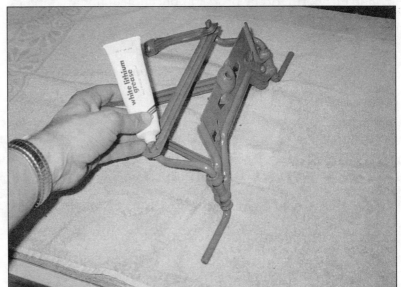

Slide the rear free wheel onto the rear axle assembly

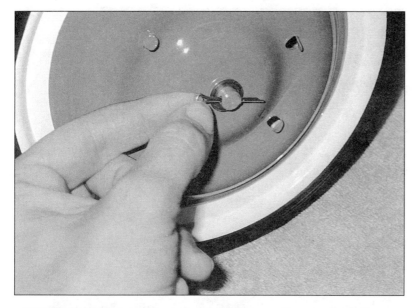

The wheel is secured with a washer and a cotter pin

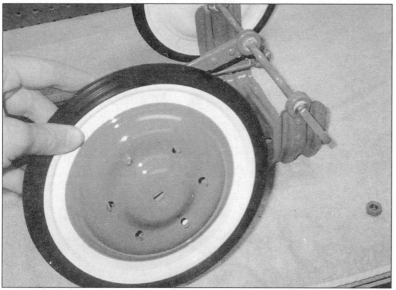

Next, the drive wheel is slid onto the axle

With an open end wrench, tighten the nut that holds the drive wheel in place

FINAL ASSEMBLY

Pop the hubcaps in place on the rear wheels and using the end of a screwdriver covered with masking tape, carefully bend the wheel tabs to secure the hubcaps

If damage occurs to the wheel tabs during installation of the hubcaps, touch up the area with a paintbrush dipped in the wheel color

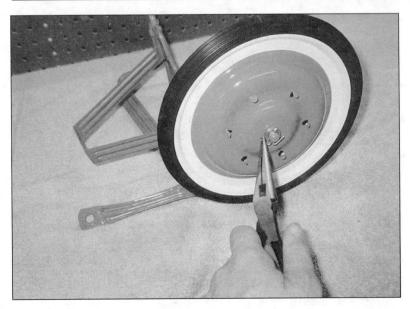

Slide the front wheels onto the front steering assembly and secure them with a washer and cotter pin

Install the front hubcaps

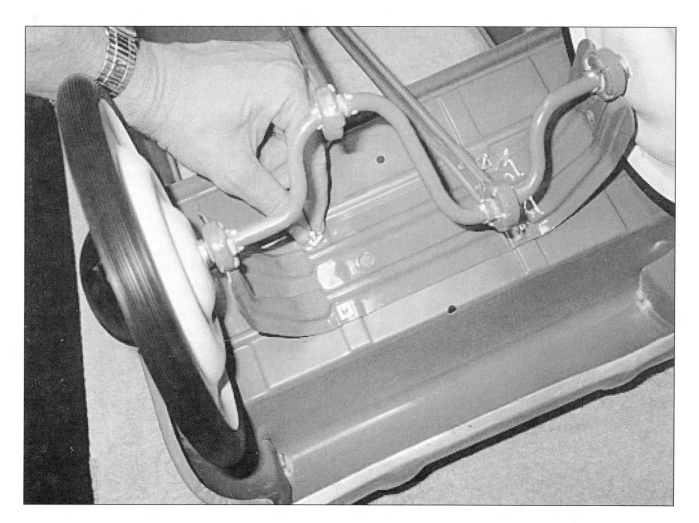

Attach the rear axle assembly to the underside of the pedal car body using four truss head screws backed with square nuts

FINAL ASSEMBLY

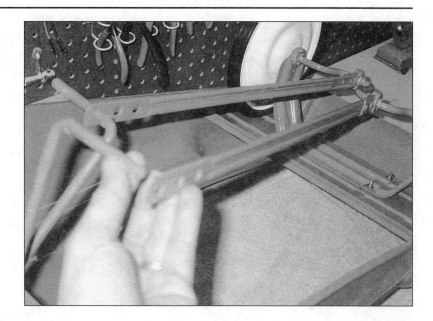

Attach the connecting straps to the pedal rods

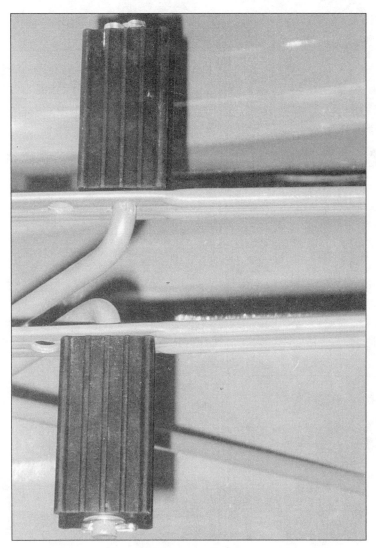

Slide the new rubber pedals onto the pedal rods and secure them with a washer and cotter pin

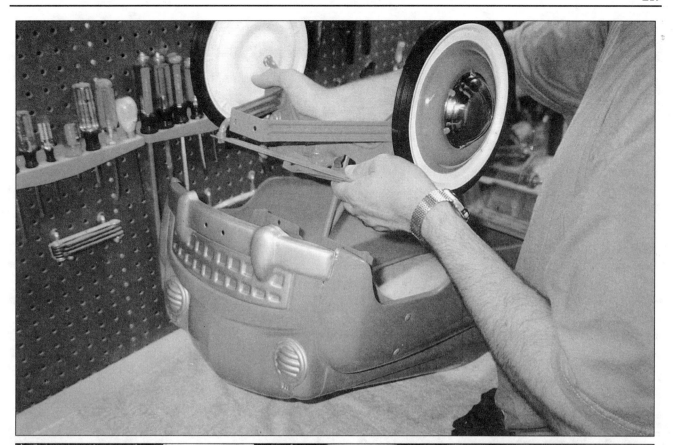

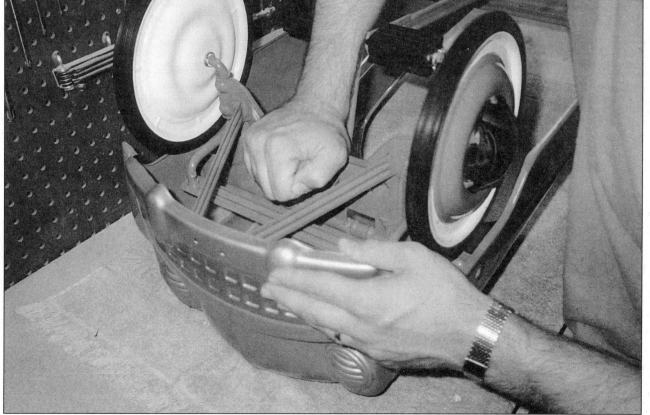

Install the front steering assembly and wheels by first placing the front brace underneath the front bumper, then firmly pushing the steering assembly into the front support

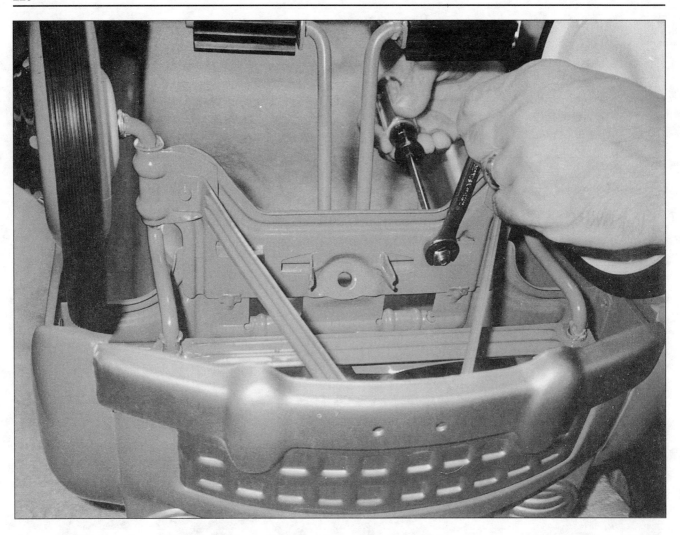

*Attach the front steering assembly to the front support
using two truss head screws and square nuts*

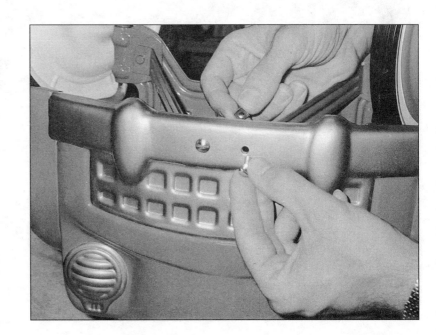

*Attach the front brace to the front bumper with
two truss head screws and square nuts*

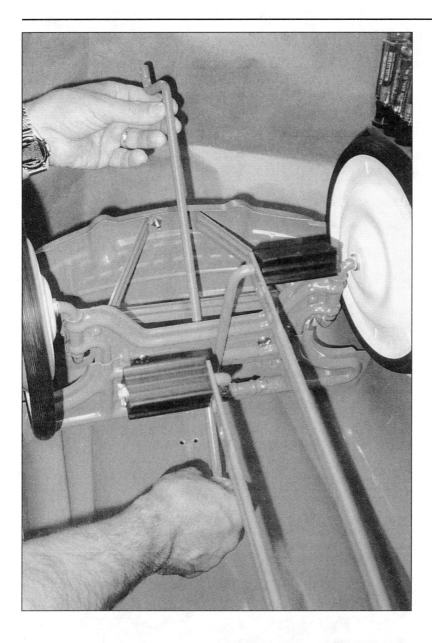

Slide the steering shaft through the front steering assembly

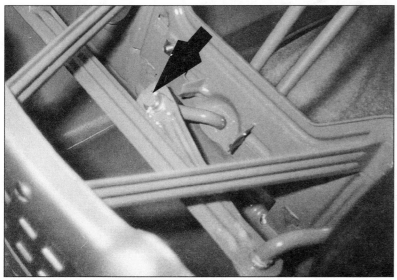

Secure the curved end of the steering shaft to the steering link using a washer and cotter pin

Place the front tab of the windshield into the slot on the hood

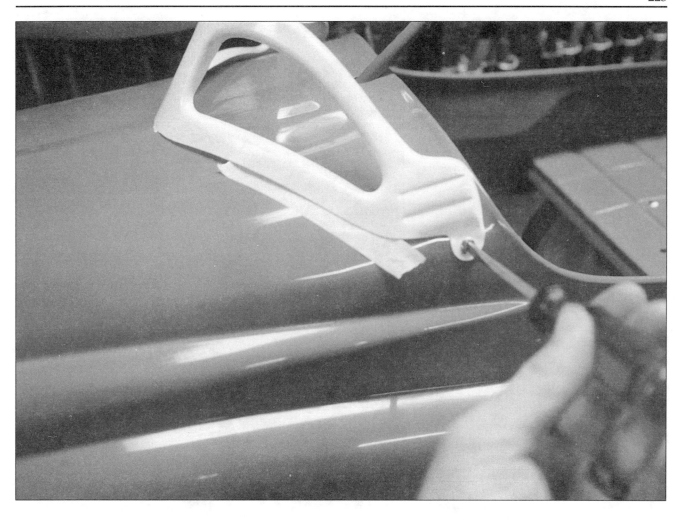

Lay down a piece of painter's masking tape to protect the hood while positioning the windshield and install the windshield with a screw and acorn nut on each side

Attach the steering wheel to the steering shaft and secure with an acorn nut

FINAL ASSEMBLY

Apply the seat label in the original location

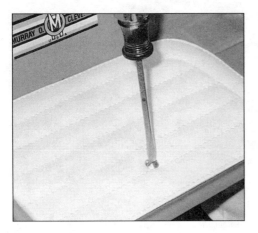

Install the seat pad by securing it to the body with a truss head screw and a nut

Add the final piece of trim, the airplane hood ornament, by inserting the tabs on the tail of the ornament into the mounting holes on the hood and securing the front of the ornament with a small machine screw

The final step is the application of the side graphics to the pedal car body

PEDAL CAR PARTS AND INFORMATION DIRECTORY

C & N Reproductions
1341 Ashover Court
Bloomfield Hills, MI 48304
810-852-1998   Pedal plane and Torpedo/Comet parts

Cowboys & Kidillacs
1709 St. Cecilia
Kingsville, TX 78363
512-595-1015   General line of parts
Owner: Allen Wilson   Best source for Garton Kidillac

Crooked Herman's
2924 Bonacum Drive
Lincoln, NE 68502
402-423-4441   Excellent source for prewar and
Owner: Ron Doan   hard to find parts

Our Gang
1991 Milton
Riverside, CA 92507
909-788-0871
Owner: Tom Perez   Show quality restorations

Portell Restorations
1574 Saddle Drive
Festus, MO 63028
314-937-8192   Good selection of prewar parts
Owner: Dan Portell   and hood ornaments

Pedal Car Accessory's
246 W. Aliso Street
Pomona, CA 91768
909-629-7153   Good prices and quality on wheels,
Owner: Van Eden   tires, pedals, and hubcaps

Pedal Car Graphics
1207 Charter Oak Drive
Taylors, SC 29687
803-244-4308
Owner: Bob Ellsworth

Complete selection of quality
pedal car graphics

Pedal Car Kid's
1512 Glenwood
Glendale, CA 91201
818-242-0378
Owners: Cliff and Lucy Cooney

"Kids" for your pedal car display
Custom dressing is also available

Noel Barrett Antiques &
   Auctions Ltd.
P.O. Box 1001
Carversville, PA 18913
215-297-5109
Owner: Noel Barrett

Full service auction house with
wheel goods experience

Samuelson Pedal Tractor Parts
619 Main Street
Box 460
Jewell, Iowa 50130
515-827-5691
Owner: Wayne Samuelson

Best source for pedal tractor
parts

Texas Pedal Car Peddler
213 Stone Drive
Fort Worth, TX 76108
817-238-8363
Owner: J. D. Dorsey

Big catalog featuring a large
selection of pedal car parts

Wheel Goods Trader
P.O. Box 435
Fraser, MI 48026-0435
810-949-6282
Publisher: John Rastall

National monthly magazine for
pedal car collectors
Reprints of old pedal car catalogs

Whim Whams
6930 Amboy
Dearborn Heights, MI 48127
313-561-2318
Owner: Andrew Gurka

Pedal car and toy restorations
"Fake rivets"

REFERENCES

Alford, Bobby. *History of Murray Ohio.* Murray, 25th Anniversary 1956-1981. Lawrenceburg, TN: Murray Ohio Manufacturing Co., 1981.

Burness, Tad. *Monstrous American Car Spotter's Guide, 1920-1980.* Osceola, WI: Motorbooks International, 1986.

"C.A. Sidway Dies from Pneumonia In New York." *Elkhart Truth.* 4 June 1915.

Caro, Joseph J. "For the Fun of It." *Toy Collector and Price Guide* 5 (August 1994): 40-43.

Consumer Guide. *Cars of the 40's.* Publications International Ltd., 1979.

Crilley, R. and C. Burkholder. *Model Farm Tractors.* West Chester, PA: Schiffer Publishing, 1985.

Dean, Paul. "Kidillacs and Fire Trucks - Pedal Cars Just Might Roll into Their Own Place in History." *The Toledo Blade,* 16 September 1983.

Diemer, Walter. Radio address. WSPD, Toledo. 21 November 1935.

Dittlinger, Esther. *Anderson: A Pictorial History.* 1990.

"Famous Old Downtown Landmark, Gendron Wheel Plant, to Be Abandoned." *Toledo Times.* 26 June 1938.

Forkner, John L. *History of Madison County.* 1914.

"Forward Edition." *Elkhart Truth.* June 1915, page 9.

REFERENCES

Gunnell, John A. *100 Years of American Cars*. Iola, WI: Krause Publications, 1993.

Jailer, Mildred. "In Their Merry Little Automobiles." *Antiques & Collecting* (November 1986): 40-43.

Kelley, Dale P. "The Pedal Car Part 1-5." *Auction Preview*. 1980.

Leberman. "History of Garton Toy Company." *One Hundred Years of Sheboygan*.

Lucey, Charles T. "Gendron Wheel Co. Is Santa Claus to World." *News-Bee*. 23 May 1927.

Marwick, Al. "The Pedal Car, Every Boy's Dream." *Old Cars Weekly News & Marketplace* (2 May 1978): 22-23.

Massucci, Edoardo. *Cars for Kids*. New York: Rizzoli International, 1983.

Motor Vehicle Manufacturers Association. *Automobiles of America*. Detroit: Wayne State University Press, 1974.

Olney/Richland County Sesquicentennial 1841 to 1991. 1991.

Pennell, Paul. *Children's Cars*. Shire Publications Ltd., 1986.

Rae, John B. *The American Automobile, A Brief History*. Chicago: University of Chicago Press, 1965.

Rinker, Harry L. "Pedaling Pedal Cars." *Antiques & Collecting* (March 1990).

Saunders, Richard. "Pedal Cars." *Americana Magazine* (April 1991): 33-35.

Smith, M. and N. Black. *America on Wheels*. William Morrow & Co., 1986.

Trumm, E. and R. A. Zarse. *Guide to Collecting Pedal Tractors and Accessories*. Worthington, IA, 1988.

Truth Publishing Co. "Sidway Mercantile Company." Elkhart 1910: 24-25.

Van Tassel, C. S. "Men Who Made Toledo." *The Toledo Blade*. 30 October 1936.

"Wheel Firm Plans Move to Archbold." *The Toledo Blade*. 1 May 1959.

Wilson, Paul C. *Chrome Dreams: Automobile Styling Since 1893.* Radnor, PA: Chilton Book Company, 1976.

Wood, Neil S. *Evolution of the Pedal Car - 1884-1970's.* Gas City, IN: L-W Book Sales, 1989.

Wood, Neil S. *Evolution of the Pedal Car,* Volume 2. Gas City, IN: L-W Book Sales, 1990.

Wood, Neil S. *Evolution of the Pedal Car,* Volume 3. Gas City, IN: L-W Book Sales, 1992.

Wood, Neil S. *Evolution of the Pedal Car,* Volume 4. Gas City, IN: L-W Book Sales, 1993.

INDEX

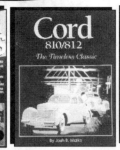    
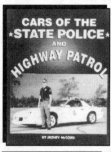     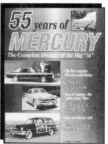
 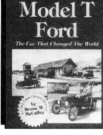 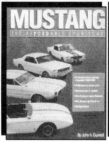   

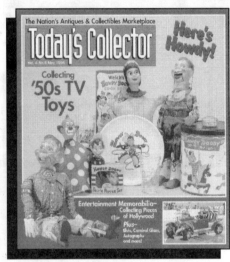
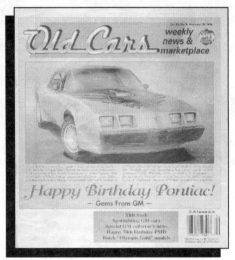